A Wife's Guide to

In-laws

How to Gain Your Husband's Loyalty
Without Killing His Parents

Written and illustrated
By
Jenna D. Barry

Lulu Publishing
Copyright © by Jenna D. Barry 2008

A Wife's Guide to In-laws
ISBN: 978-0-557-02500-8

by Lulu, Inc.
www.Lulu.com

TABLE OF CONTENTS

ACKNOWLEDGEMENTS

To my wonderful husband: Thank you for having the courage to make me your first priority.

To Mom: Even though you wrote so many corrections on my manuscript that I briefly considered setting it on fire, you are the best cheerleader a daughter could ask for.

To my "best good girlfriend" and her rock star husband: Thank you for editing my manuscript, and helping with my marketing plan.

To Dr. Scott Haltzman: Thank you for being the first person besides my own mother who liked my book. You have been a huge encouragement to me!

To Carole Greene: Thank you for all your help with my book, and for believing it will help a lot of people.

INTRODUCTION

They say married couples usually fight about these 3 things: sex, money, and in-laws. I'm fortunate enough to be married to someone who basically shares my viewpoint on sex (we both like it) and money (we both like to spend it). But when it comes to in-laws, we had approximately 3.7 million arguments in the first five years of marriage alone.

You may be quick to blame your in-laws for your marriage problems, but in reality the biggest part of the problem isn't really your in-laws, it's your husband's loyalty to them. When a man marries, he is supposed to transfer his loyalty from his parents to his wife. His behavior plays a key role in how well you get along with his parents. The goal of this book is to help you gain your husband's loyalty.

A Wife's Guide to In-laws is written from the perspective of a wife with difficult in-laws and a husband whose loyalties are divided. However, I realize that (1) not all in-laws are difficult, (2) not all husbands are disloyal, (3) sometimes it's the wife, not the husband, who has trouble transferring loyalty, and (4) sometimes it's the wife's parents, not the husband's parents, who are difficult.

You *don't* need to read this book if...
- you have wonderful in-laws
- you have a loyal husband who makes your needs a priority (even if it upsets his parents)

You *do* need to read this book if...
- you have self-centered, manipulative in-laws
- your husband frequently makes his parents' needs a priority over yours
- your main goal is to have a fantastic relationship with your husband

Although the goal of this book is not to help you have a terrific relationship with your in-laws, your relationship with them will likely improve automatically once your husband makes you his #1 priority.

Chapter 1

Something Smells Fishy
Evaluating your in-laws' destructive behavior

You're gonna need a bigger boat.
--Roy Scheider as Police Chief Martin
Brody in the movie <u>Jaws</u> *1975*

W hen a preacher says "for better or for worse" he is talking about in-laws. He won't come right out and say that because they are sitting right there, but that's what he means. Like it or not, when you marry, your husband is part of a package deal.[1]

Wouldn't it have been great if, on your wedding day, your in-laws would have come up to you and said, "We realize you are independent adults with a life of your own. We know your first priority belongs to each other now instead of to us. Please tell us whenever we say or do anything that causes tension in your marriage so we can change our behavior." I know this didn't happen to you because if it did, you wouldn't be reading this book. A more realistic scenario of what happened as you drove away in a car covered with JUST MARRIED decorations was that your husband's parents were knee-deep in what I call the Adjustment Stage...the time to let go of their grown son so he can transfer his loyalty to his spouse. Now concentrate because this next sentence contains large words *and* some math. <u>The degree to which a woman will get along with her in-laws is indirectly proportional to how long they remain in the Adjustment Stage.</u> In other words, the more

---

[1] I realize there are a lot of wonderful, loving in-laws whose behavior doesn't cause any tension toward their son's marriage. However, I have chosen not to discuss them in this book because it was written for women with difficult in-laws.

quickly parents learn to let go of their son, the better they will get along with his wife.

My husband's parents have been in the Adjustment Stage for more than a decade. Therefore, it is mathematically impossible for me to like them. But just because I don't like them doesn't mean I can't have a decent, respectful relationship with them. And more importantly, just because I don't like them doesn't mean I can't have a great relationship with my husband. The same goes for you.

It's important to realize that a lot of in-laws have a bad reputation even though some aren't as horrible as everybody thinks. Whale sharks struggle with the same stereotype.

I saw an episode about them on television a while ago. They are huge and seem scary until you learn they don't eat people, just plankton. Their teeth are tiny and useless. That's why you don't see anybody making horror movies about whale sharks. I suppose if you wanted to make a horror movie for the plankton population, a whale shark would make a great main character, but that's beside the point. Take a look at the three categories below and evaluate whether or not your in-laws fit the descriptions. If so, then it's possible your in-laws aren't as harmful as you think.

WHALE SHARK IN-LAWS: TYPE 1

These in-laws have absolutely no idea their behavior hurts you and they would be sad to learn that it did. While you are seething with anger, they may be totally oblivious to the fact that they are a source of tension in your marriage. It may be obvious to *you* that they trample over your needs as a couple, but they may not realize it. Chances are, if you respectfully let them know how you want them to behave, they will be gracious, humble, and willing to change. There is great potential for having a good relationship with these in-laws.

WHALE SHARK IN-LAWS: TYPE 2

These in-laws can sense that their behavior upsets you but they don't know what to do about it. They are willing to change but don't know how. They will keep behaving in their old familiar pattern until someone (you and/or your husband) teaches them a new behavior pattern in a respectful way. There is great potential for having a good relationship with these in-laws too.

WHALE SHARK IN-LAWS: TYPE 3

These in-laws are aware that they are hurting you. They know how to change and are trying to change, but they need a little more time. They're still in the process of replacing old, unhealthy behaviors with new, healthy ones. It can be hard to distinguish this type of whale shark in-law from the more dangerous great whites (which I will discuss later in the chapter) because you can't read their minds...all you see is their actions. If your in-laws fit into this category, chances are they will improve their behavior if you are persistent in (1) respectfully communicating your needs and (2) offering them praise whenever they make an effort to respect those needs. There is great potential for having a good relationship with these in-laws.

Now it's time to talk about the sharks who *have* earned their poor reputation. That's right, I'm talking about the great white shark from the movie Jaws. I don't think anyone would argue if I called him a jerk. After all, he went around devouring all those nice people who were minding their own business.[2]

---

[2] I still can't swim in pools at night.

Some in-laws are jerks too. They can pose a very real threat to your marriage. It's important to learn as much as you can about them so you can protect yourself and your marriage. Do any of the following categories describe your in-laws?

NOT-SO-GREAT WHITE SHARK IN-LAWS: TYPE 1

These in-laws are aware that their behavior is hurting you and your marriage. They know they *should* change and they know *how* to change, but they don't *want* to change. Their relationship with their son is more important to them than the success of his marriage. Chances are, if you respectfully let them know how you need them to behave, they will overreact in order to get you to back down. They may accuse you of trying to keep them from their son. They may use your tactful confrontation as a way to draw pity from their son and turn him against you. They may twist your words and say you were mean to them. They may even tell your husband he needs to choose between you and them.

If you can learn ways to prevent them from turning your husband against you whenever you confront them, these in-laws aren't as dangerous as you might think.[3] If you hold your ground as they sulk,

---

[3] I'll discuss this more in the chapter called "We Don't Need No Stinking Boundaries."

pout, whine, cry and blame, they will probably change their behavior, although they'll complain about having to do so. There is not much potential for having a good relationship with these in-laws because, even if they do change their behavior, they will always view you as a newcomer intent on ruining their relationship with their son. Unless your husband unites with you in setting and enforcing boundaries, your relationship with them will continue to be less than pleasant. [4]

○ NOT SO GREAT WHITE SHARK IN-LAWS: TYPE 2

These in-laws are aware that they are hurting you but they don't want to acknowledge that because it would ruin their superficial image of being perfect parents. Their unhealthy behavior is a product of fear and insecurity. They pretend their relationship with you is fine in order to avoid appearing weak, flawed, and vulnerable. They cling to familiar behavior patterns they have used for years instead of admitting change is necessary. These in-laws *say* they want a better relationship with you, but they ignore every suggestion you give on how to change their behavior. They refuse to respect your boundaries and then complain to their son that they can't understand why you don't like them. They tell him they have tried their best but still don't know how to win you over. They try to make it look as though *they* are making a gallant effort to have a loving relationship, but *you* aren't trying at all. They try to convince him they are good, loving parents and you are a hateful daughter-in-law. By making subtle negative comments about you, they teach their son that it's more important to be their confidante than a loyal husband.

Caution must be used when confronting this type of in-law about their unhealthy behavior.[5] It can be extremely difficult to maintain control of a verbal confrontation with them because they have very subtle ways of controlling conversations. This type of in-law has mastered the art of manipulation with and without words. It won't be easy to see through their superficial words or pinpoint what is really being said through a lifted eyebrow or a certain tone of voice. It will be impossible to defend yourself against their manipulation until you learn how to confront their

---

[4] See page 22 for the definition of boundaries.
[5] I'll give tips on how to confront this type of in-law in the chapter called "We Don't Need No Stinking Boundaries."

hidden messages. If you tell them what your needs are, they will view it as a personal attack. Instead of apologizing for overlooking your needs, they will focus on how *you* are hurting them by having needs that conflict with theirs. Or they may offer a superficial, insincere apology while at the same time denying any wrongdoing by saying you misunderstood them or they were just kidding. Regardless of which method they use, their goal is to maintain their saintly image while making you look like the bad guy.

In-laws who fit into this category have no intention of making an effort to learn whether or not their behavior is appropriate. They probably won't read books or talk to a counselor, much less listen to you. They're uninformed and want to stay that way because discovering the truth might allow others to see their flaws. That doesn't mean you shouldn't try to challenge the false beliefs dictating their behavior. Nor does it mean you should stop communicating your needs to them. Regardless of whether or not they change their unhealthy behavior, you can protect your marriage by setting boundaries. The rest of this book will teach you how.

NOT-SO-GREAT WHITE SHARK IN-LAWS: TYPE 3

These in-laws are too arrogant and self-centered to concern themselves with whether or not their behavior hurts you. They are behaving the way they always have, and they have absolutely no intention of changing. They are so consumed with their position of superiority that they aren't concerned with your needs, nor those of your husband. They firmly believe that it is their *right* as parents to be the ones in charge. They think because they have done so much for you, you *owe* it to them to do anything they want you to do. They expect you to revolve your world around them.

Chances are, even if you and your husband communicate your needs a million times in a united, respectful, loving way, they will no sooner change their behavior than pull watermelons out of their nostrils. Whenever they sense you becoming more difficult to control, they will try even harder to maintain that control. If you confront them about their destructive behavior, they will say you are overreacting and being too sensitive. They may accuse you and/or your husband of being rude, selfish, and disrespectful. They may gang up on you in order to remain in power. (For example, your husband's mom may accuse him of being disrespectful to his father. Or your husband's father may accuse him of hurting his mom's feelings.) They may try to convince you that honest confrontation is a bad thing by making false statements such as, "People who love each other should overlook each other's flaws (instead of acknowledging hurts and working through them)." The closest thing you will get to an apology from them is, "We are just trying to help you become a better person," but this is just a lousy excuse for controlling you.

It's extremely important that you learn how to see through their faulty thinking and teach your husband to do the same so they will no longer be a threat to your marriage.[6] Since it is unlikely that anything you say will convince them to change their behavior, your best bet is to enforce boundaries without wasting your time explaining to them why you aren't going to let them control your life anymore.

Now that you have read this chapter, which type of in-laws do you think you have...the type that just swim around sucking in plankton or the ones that will rip your legs off? If your in-laws fit into one of the more harmful categories, then this book was written especially for you.

---

[6] I'll discuss this more in the chapter called "Stop Making That Face or It Will Get Stuck that Way."

Don't spend too much time trying to figure out which category your in-laws fit into. It's okay if they don't fit neatly into one category on all issues. Just try to learn and apply what you can and keep in mind that in-laws can change from one type to another. It's entirely possible that you may not be able to determine which type they are until after you have applied some of the strategies from this book. The more familiar you are with your in-law's destructive behavior patterns, the better prepared you will be to cope with them and gain your husband's loyalty.

A WIFE'S GUIDE TO IN-LAWS

Chapter 2

Shark Bait No More
Changing your false thinking and unhealthy behavior

*The sign of an intelligent people is their ability to
control emotions by the application of reason.*
                                                --Mayra Mannes

Whenever I hear the song "Africa,"[1] I sing along at the top of my lungs. Recently I discovered I have been singing the wrong lyrics for over 20 years. It turns out the line "There's nothing that a hundred men on Mars could ever do" is actually "There's nothing that a hundred men *or more* could ever do." Once I learned that my original thinking was wrong, I substituted correct thinking in its place. In other words, my behavior improved after I changed my thinking. I stopped singing about Martians. And if you ask my husband, he'll tell you the world is a little bit better place now.

I'll bet you are absolutely certain about some things that are completely wrong. And that faulty thinking has a huge, negative impact on your behavior. Although your husband's parents probably can't detect blood from several miles away as sharks can, they can detect your weaknesses by your reactions. If you generally overreact or underreact to situations involving your in-laws, then your unhealthy behavior may actually be *inviting* their attacks. This chapter will help you evaluate the flaws in your current thinking so your behavior will improve, making you less vulnerable to your in-laws.

---

[1] By the band, Toto.

One way you encourage your in-laws to "attack" you is by having a negative view of yourself and your situation. This unhealthy thinking can destroy your ability to bring about positive change. When you think about your in-laws and their effect on your marriage, how do you feel? Do you feel helpless, scared and alone? Do you feel betrayed, violated, and unimportant? Do you feel frustrated, powerless, and unsure? Do you feel guilty, misjudged, and trapped? Do you feel angry, guarded, and out of control? Do you feel lost, discouraged, and defeated?

Have you ever stopped to ask yourself why you've developed such a negative view of yourself and your situation? It's possible your in-laws (and husband) have said and done things to make you think you are a bad person...or that you are powerless to change anything. Maybe they have accused you of being selfish whenever your needs conflicted with theirs. Perhaps they have called you disrespectful whenever you tried to set reasonable limits with them. Maybe they said you were being paranoid when you caught them gossiping about you. Perhaps they accused you of being overly sensitive whenever their teasing got out of hand.

The problem with us human beings is that sometimes, if we are around other people long enough, we start to believe what they say, even if they are wrong. We can't remember what we were like before their destructive behavior taught us to doubt our own beliefs and opinions. If you have let your in-laws (and husband) convince you that you are selfish, disrespectful, paranoid, and overly sensitive, then you need a more accurate perception of yourself. Otherwise you won't have the confidence needed to protect yourself or your marriage.

Your negative thinking is probably affecting your behavior in a way that causes you to underreact or overreact whenever you interact with your in-laws.

Underreacting is a product of unhealthy thinking. It's a result of having a negative view of yourself and your situation. It's when you assume it's normal and acceptable to allow others to overlook your needs and violate your boundaries. Underreacting is when you decide something is not worth dealing with because you don't think anything will ever change.

Underreacting is when you wait for others to solve your problems instead of doing what is in your power to do. It's when you decide not to do anything because you don't want to upset your husband again. It's when you tell yourself that anything you do will make things worse. It's when you take the easy way out in the short term, which ends up making things worse in the long term. It's when you convince yourself it's better to stay miserable than to take control of your life. It's when you decide it's better to let your marriage slowly dissolve than experience the discomfort involved in bringing about change.

To put it in simple terms, when you underreact, you are being a pansy. People who underreact usually have some or all of these false beliefs:

- If I decide to do something *I* want to do instead of what my husband/in-laws want me to do, I am selfish.
- In order to be a good daughter-in-law, I must do everything my in-laws want me to do.
- I owe it to my in-laws to let them violate my boundaries because they are "family."
- I am responsible for their happiness.
- If they are upset with me, it's because I did something wrong or selfish.
- I should always drop what I'm doing in order to accommodate my in-laws so I don't upset them.
- Their opinions, wants, and needs are superior to mine because they are older than me.
- My in-laws have the right to decide how I should spend my time and money.

- It would be disrespectful for me to confront them about their unhealthy behavior.
- It's my husband's job, not mine, to confront his parents and draw boundaries.[2]
- In order to be a loving person, I have to let others treat me poorly.
- It's better to avoid the truth and have superficial relationships than to tell the truth and have genuine relationships.

If you do any of these things on a regular basis, then you are underreacting:

- You ignore your feelings and keep them bottled up inside.
- You do what your in-laws want you to do instead of doing what *you* want to do.
- You ignore your needs so you won't upset them.
- You don't confront them when their behavior hurts you or your marriage.
- You question your decisions when they don't agree with you.
- You accept their version of reality over your own.
- You blame yourself for things that aren't your fault.

Every time you underreact, you encourage your in-laws to continue treating you the same way. If you keep your feelings bottled up instead of confronting them, they are unlikely to change their behavior. If you always do what your in-laws want without considering what *you* want, then you are teaching them that what you want isn't important. When you ignore your needs so you don't upset your in-laws, you teach them that it's better for *you* to be upset than for *them* to be upset. When you question decisions your in-laws don't approve of, then you unnecessarily keep yourself in an inferior position.

If you accept their version of reality over your own (for instance they say they are just kidding about something you know they are serious about), you are telling yourself you aren't capable of determining what is really going on in a certain situation. When you apologize for things that

---

[2] In a perfect world, if a man's parents have inappropriate behavior, then it is his job to confront them himself. It is less awkward for parents when they are challenged by their own son, rather than by their daughter-in-law. Unfortunately many men refuse to stand up to their parents. In those cases, it's better for the daughter-in-law to confront them rather than no one standing up to them at all.

aren't your fault, you are saying that *you* are the one with unhealthy behavior. As a result, your in-laws get to maintain an image of perfection instead of dealing with their unhealthy behavior. Speaking the truth in love can be a form of integrity; it gives the people who hurt you a chance to change their unhealthy behavior.

Maybe underreacting isn't a problem for you. Perhaps, instead, you struggle with overreacting. *Overreacting* is when you take everything personally and don't let anyone get close to you. It's when you're in a constant state of defensiveness. It's when you assume the worst about everyone and never give them the benefit of the doubt. It's when your goal is to appear so tough and inflexible that your in-laws are too scared of your wrath to challenge you.

Overreacting is when you think the only way to survive your situation is to repay evil for evil. It's when you stoop to the level of the immature, ignorant people around you. It's when you set rigid, harsh boundaries in order to punish your in-laws. It's when you say and do things just to spite them. It's when you allow your rage to dictate the way you treat others. It's when you escalate the tension in a situation instead of helping to defuse it. It's when you say and do things in the heat of the moment that you'll later regret, instead of maintaining control of your emotions. It's when you insist on always being right instead of behaving in a fair, respectful, and loving way. It's when you control and retaliate against others instead of keeping in mind the long-term goal of gaining your husband's loyalty. To put it in simple terms, overreacting is getting your panties in a wad.

People who overreact usually have some or all of these false beliefs:

- Everyone is at fault except me; my behavior is perfect.
- My in-laws should change *their* behavior; *my* behavior is perfectly fine.
- Things will improve only if they change their behavior; I don't have the ability to make positive changes without their cooperation.
- I should try to convince them that I'm not selfish or disrespectful.
- My in-laws must agree with all of my decisions and approve all of my actions.
- Any day now they will realize my needs are important and their behavior is unacceptable.
- I will win my husband's loyalty by blaming his parents for all of my problems.

If you do any of the following on a regular basis, then you are overreacting:

- You blame your in-laws for all of your relationship problems.
- You insist they change their behavior before you'll consider changing yours.
- You try to convince them to perceive things the same way you do.
- You behave immaturely during conversations with them (ex: slam doors, cuss, scream, make accusations, threaten, criticize, spit, etc.)
- You gossip about them instead of confronting them directly in a respectful manner.
- You intentionally do things to upset them whenever they do something to upset you.

Every time you overreact, (1) you do not take advantage of the real power you have to improve your situation and (2) you don't give your husband any reason to want to transfer his loyalty to you. Whenever you gossip about your in-laws, you may *think* you're tough but actually you lack the courage to confront them directly. If you behave immaturely during conversations with them, then you embolden them to treat you with that same immaturity. And when you try to convince them to see things the same way you do, you are actually saying you desperately need their approval. If you think you are stuck in your situation unless your in-laws change *their* behavior, then you sentence yourself to remain a victim.

It's usually best to discuss problems directly with the people involved, such as your husband or his parents. However, if you are too angry to speak in a respectful tone to them, then you may need to vent your feelings to someone else. Be very careful about who you vent to! If you need to complain about your in-laws, don't vent to your husband (because that will make him less likely to transfer his loyalty to you). Don't complain to your own family either, because that will create tension between your family, your husband, and his parents.

If you need to complain about your husband, don't vent to your family because they will still be mad at him long after you've forgiven him. Don't vent about Hubby to his family either; that's disrespectful to him, and besides, his family will probably defend him (their loyalty is with him, not you). You wouldn't want him to complain to your parents about you, so show him the same respect. Avoid telling your mutual friends or girlfriends too.

Here's who you CAN tell: a "safe person." A safe person should be someone like a counselor or pastor. It should be a mature person (preferably of your same gender) who helps to dissolve your anger, rather than intensify it. Your safe person should help you brainstorm respectful things to say/do to set and enforce boundaries with your husband and his parents. At your request, I can try to pair you up with another wife if you go to my website (www.WifeGuide.org) and join my support group. For a list of marriage professionals who support the ideas in my book, please visit my website. (If you are a marriage professional who would like to be referred on my website, please read the note in the Conclusion.)

The problems you have with them can be resolved whether or not your in-laws change their unhealthy behavior. You just need to learn how to modify your own behavior in order to achieve the results you want. You have the power to take control of your life instead of waiting around in vain for other people to come to their senses.

You may tend to overreact if you don't know how to deal with that red hot, burning feeling that consumes you whenever your in-laws say or do certain things. Anger can be a useful emotion that tells you when you are being violated so that you will do something about it. When you feel angry with your in-laws, it's probably because they crossed the line of what is and isn't appropriate or respectful. You are *supposed* to feel angry when your in-laws violate your need for time, space, privacy, etc. Regardless of what others tell you, you're not a horrible person just because you get angry. You're a human being. Everybody gets angry. If you didn't get angry it would mean you were in a coma or dead. BUT just because it's normal to feel angry doesn't mean you should feel free to release your anger however you want to.

There are healthy ways to deal with anger, and then there are unhealthy ways. Take Mike Tyson for example. Biting off someone's ear is not a healthy way to deal with anger. If you asked Lorena Bobbitt's husband to give you an example of an unhealthy way to deal with anger, I bet he could come up with one.[3] Likewise, screaming "YOU STINK!!!" as you drive by your in-laws' house is not an appropriate way. Sure, you'll feel instant gratification but in the end it will just make your husband less motivated to transfer his loyalty to you. After all, who wants to give his loyalty to a crazy woman? When you come across looking like an enraged lunatic, your husband is more likely to join sides with his parents who have mastered the art of looking like perfect angels.

The first few seconds of being consumed with anger can be the most difficult to handle. That's the time when it's best to head straight toward the nearest roll of duct tape and secure it firmly over your mouth. Then excuse yourself (to the bathroom or to London) for as long as it takes for you to gain control of your emotions[4]. Only then should you remove the duct tape and speak as calmly and respectfully as possible. The extent to which your in-laws can push your buttons is the degree to which they still have power over you. Learn what your buttons are and brainstorm new responses. In the future, if they push your buttons and don't get the same response out of you, then they no longer have power over you.

Another great way to deal with your anger is to do what is in your power to prevent the situations that make you angry in the first place. In other words, you can communicate your needs, set boundaries, and enforce boundaries. I'll discuss this in more detail throughout the rest of the book.

---

[3] Remember the poor dude whose wife cut off his zippity doo dah?

[4] While you are there you can scream into a pillow, stomp on bubble wrap, complain to your pet iguana, or write a nasty letter to your in-laws and then burn it without giving it to them.

A couple of years ago, my friend's three year-old-daughter looked up at me and asked, "Did you grow up yet?" I didn't know how to answer her question. Sure, I was married. I owned a house. I had a job. I paid bills. I paid taxes. But had I really grown up? The truth was that in many ways I hadn't. In some ways I still thought of myself as a child, and therefore, so did other people. . . especially my in-laws.

Do you view yourself as an adult, on an equal status level with your in-laws? When your in-laws say or do something you find inappropriate, do you respond as an adult? Or do you respond as a child?

Here's a scenario to help you understand the point I'm trying to make. Let's say your 12-year-old son walked into your room when you happened to be buck-naked. How would you react? Would you cry? Would you scream? Would you be furious at your son? Would you blame your husband for allowing your son to treat you like this? Would you blame your son for being nosey and intrusive? Would you tell everyone you know what a horrible son you have because he doesn't respect your boundaries? Would you go into a state of depression because you don't have privacy in your bedroom? If so, then you would be responding as if you were a child. These reactions probably seem ridiculous in this scenario. But I bet you'll understand my point if you reread this paragraph, only this time imagine it was your in-laws—instead of your son—who walked in on you. Now those reactions don't seem so far fetched, do they?

If your son barged into your bedroom, the proper adult response would be to (1) communicate your needs, (2) set a boundary, and (3) enforce your boundary. You could communicate your needs and set a boundary by saying in a calm, respectful tone "I need some privacy, Honey. From now on I expect you to knock, and then wait until someone opens the door instead of just walking into our bedroom." You could then enforce your boundary by locking your bedroom door whenever you wanted privacy. By enforcing your boundary, you would be able to protect yourself whether or not your son changed his behavior.

This is how you need to deal with your in-laws when problem situations arise. Since your in-laws' behavior can be like that of a child, then you need to be the mature adult. A mature response is not to cry, scream, gossip, blame, or complain when they behave in an unhealthy manner. A mature response is to (1) communicate your needs in a respectful manner, (2) set a boundary, and (3) enforce the boundary.

The next time your in-laws do something that upsets you, respond as if they were children with inappropriate behavior. I'm not saying you should talk down to them in a belittling manner. Nor am I suggesting that you are on a level superior to your in-laws. You are actually on an equal level with them. But imagining your in-laws as children may help you realize the extent to which you view them as superior. Here's another scenario to help illustrate my point. Let's say you and your husband are shopping for furniture with your mother-in-law. You and Hubby find a sofa you love, and you tell the salesman you'd like to buy it. But then your mother-in-law starts shaking her head disapprovingly and tells you she doesn't like the color you picked. She tries to talk you into a sofa that is "more in your price range."

How would you respond to her in that situation? Would you try to suffocate her with throw pillows? Would you glare at your husband, resenting him for not telling his mom to go to hell? Or would you go to the other extreme and agree to buy an ugly, cheap sofa because you think maybe your mother-in-law is right? Now what if you were to look at this scenario from a different angle? This time imagine you and your husband are out shopping for furniture with your 10-year-old daughter. You find a sofa you love and your husband tells the salesman you'd like to buy it. But then your daughter starts shaking her head disapprovingly and tells you she doesn't like the color you picked and tries to talk you into a sofa that is "more in your price range."

How would you respond? Would you feel violated by her intrusive comments? Would you demand that your husband tell her to leave the store? Or would you simply dismiss her comments and say, "You're entitled to your opinion, but this is the one your dad and I have decided to buy"?

If you don't like it when your in-laws treat you like a child, then stop LETTING them treat you like one. The best way to do that is to start behaving as an adult. Here's a test to help you determine whether or not you view yourself on the same level as your in-laws. First, read and answer the following questions the way they are written. When you are done with that, then go through and answer them again, but imagine your in-laws (instead of a child) in each of the situations. Compare the two sets of responses.

How would you respond if …

- your 4-year-old son said you were a lousy cook and didn't keep your house very clean?
- your 8-year-old son played a guilt trip on you because you wouldn't spend the holidays where he wanted?
- your 16-year-old son read your diary or mail?
- your neighbor's 9-year-old daughter frequently dropped by uninvited and expected you to spend time with her?
- your kids' friends went into your bedroom without asking your permission?
- the neighbor kid interfered in an argument between you and your husband?
- your neighbor's 7-year-old son said you weren't doing a very good job raising your kids?
- your neighbor's teenage daughter started behaving as if *your* kids were *her* kids?
- you found out your 11-year-old daughter had been gossiping about you to your husband and/or other family members?
- your daughter insisted you come visit her at college every Sunday, regardless of your needs or schedule?
- your teenage son insisted you cancel your business dinner because he needed help with his car for the fifth weekend in a row?

I keep mentioning boundaries but maybe you aren't sure what a boundary is. A *boundary* is a limit. If you set a boundary with someone, you show them how you will and will not allow yourself to be treated. The purpose of setting a boundary is not to be cruel, nor is it to punish someone (no matter how much you want to). Setting boundaries is a very necessary and wise thing to do if you want to have genuine, healthy relationships. The purpose of a boundary is to protect yourself and/or your marriage. Think of your marriage as a castle and a boundary as the moat. A moat is designed to keep the castle from being destroyed by intruders. You may not be able to change your in-laws' behavior, but you can set limits on how their behavior affects you.

False thinking has probably caused you to have unhealthy behavior in the past. The good news is from now on you can communicate your needs and draw boundaries.

Chapter 3

Marking Your Territory
Discovering your needs and setting boundaries with your in-laws

Never look at the trombones. You'll only encourage them.
--Richard Strauss, on conducting

Are you ready to set some boundaries with your in-laws? Great! Let's get started. Get a piece of paper and write a list of what your in-laws do that makes you feel upset, belittled, angry, frustrated, unimportant, or hurt[1].

I don't know what your list says, but I bet your list has some similarities to this one.

1. They call too early, too late, and too often[2].
2. They invite themselves over and drop by unannounced.
3. They beg us to come visit them all the time…especially during the holidays.
4. They give unwanted advice and meddle in things that aren't their business.
5. They control us with money.
6. They make hurtful comments and then say they're only teasing.
7. They manipulate me with hidden messages and nonverbal communication.
8. They expect me to call them "Mom" and "Dad."
9. My mother-in-law expects me to be the daughter she never had.
10. My mother-in-law gossips about me to my husband, friends, and other family members.

It's important that you don't let my list influence you to find more excuses to dislike your in-laws. For example, if you see on my list of complaints that some in-laws call too late at night…but it doesn't bother you when your in-laws call at midnight, then don't suddenly decide that you hate it when they call at midnight.

Now let's go through each item on this list one at a time in order to help you determine some appropriate boundaries to help your marriage grow stronger.

---

[1] Cross off any behavior on your list that is annoying but not destructive. For example, if you wrote that your father-in-law's breath could kill a sewer rat, then put a line through that one.

[2] Your in-laws may call, visit, and/or expect you to visit constantly because they have unmet needs in their own lives that cause them to be insecure, needy, and suffocating. Perhaps they are unhappily married, divorced, or widowed. Or maybe they have lingering effects from a traumatic childhood such as the loss of their own parent(s).

#1 *They call too early, too late, and too often.*

It's 6 AM on Saturday and your mother-in-law jumps out of bed, ready to make another day of your life a living hell. While eating her Cream O' Wheat, she realizes she has an extremely important question for the two of you. The telephone jolts you awake and somehow you manage to find the phone on the nightstand, even though it's still dark and your limbs are not yet fully functioning. "What are your plans for the 4th of July?!!" she asks excitedly as you lie in bed trying to figure out where you are and who you're talking to. Her question is a legitimate one, although probably one that could've waited until noon. It is, after all, only February.

CONSIDER THIS . . . You don't need a good excuse for not answering the phone. You aren't a bad person if you decide to screen calls from your in-laws sometimes. You don't need to feel guilty for not returning someone's call instantly every time they leave you a message.

WHAT DO *YOU* THINK? Below are some questions to help you determine your needs so you can set boundaries on this issue. Don't worry about what anyone else thinks for right now. It doesn't matter what your in-laws think. It doesn't matter what your husband thinks. It doesn't matter what your friends or co-workers think. It doesn't matter what I think. What do YOU think?

1. Do your in-laws call earlier or later than you'd like them to call? Yes   No
2. What is the earliest time in the morning you want them to call? _____ AM
3. What is the latest time at night you want them to call? _____ PM
4. Write down some activities during which you don't want to answer the phone. (For example: putting the kids to bed or exercising) _____
5. Are you a person who loves to spend hours on the phone? Yes   No
6. Do you prefer to send e-mails, write letters, or visit in person rather than talk on the phone? Yes   No

7. Do your in-laws call more often than you would like to talk to them? Yes   No
8. How often would you prefer to talk to your in-laws on the phone? Once per _____

EXAMPLES OF BOUNDARY STATEMENTS:

- From now on I will only talk with my in-laws on the phone between the hours of [9AM and 9PM].
- From now on I will not talk with my in-laws on the phone while I am doing the following activities: [cooking, eating, watching a certain TV show, entertaining guests, or sleeping].
- From now on I will primarily keep in touch with my in-laws in this way: [e-mail].
- In general, from now on I will only talk on the phone with my in-laws [2-3 times a month].

Now it's time to write some boundary statements of your own. Don't assume your boundary statements should be exactly the same as my examples. Everyone has different wants, needs, social standards, and opinions. Your boundary statements should be custom-designed for you. You can use the space below or write on a separate paper.

#2 *They invite themselves over and drop by unannounced.*

You've finally made it thorough a hectic Monday. You have a headache and you're starving. Since your hubby is working late tonight you swing through the drive-thru and order yourself a Big Mac meal. And a large chocolate shake . . .what the heck, you deserve it. You're looking forward to an evening alone so you can unwind. Maybe you'll take a long bubble bath or lounge in front of the TV with sole control of the remote. But wait…what's that in your driveway? No, not your mother-in-law's car! "I heard Mike was working late so I'm here to keep you company!" she yells from your front porch. "How nice," you mumble, just before throwing up.

CONSIDER THIS . . . You don't need to feel guilty for not answering the doorbell for guests you didn't invite in the first place. You aren't a bad person if you decide not to invite your in-laws inside when they drop by unexpectedly. You don't need a good excuse for asking them to come back at another time.

WHAT DO *YOU* THINK?

1. Do you like it when your in-laws invite themselves to your house?
   Yes   No
   If you answered yes, then how often is it okay for them to invite themselves over? Every day? Once a week? Once a month?
   February 29th? _____
2. Would you prefer they wait and let you be the one to invite them over? Yes   No
3. Do you like it when your in-laws drop by unannounced?
   Yes   No
   If you answered yes, then are there certain days (or times of the day) you prefer they *not* drop by? If so, then when?
   Before 9 AM? After dinner? Sundays? _____

If you are a newlywed then it's very important how you handle the first visit(s) with your in-laws because it will set the pattern for future visits. Behave in ways that show you are an adult and your home is your personal space. If you want to have some control over when your in-laws come over, don't let them determine the date and duration of the visit.

EXAMPLES OF BOUNDARY STATEMENTS:

- From now on I [will not] allow my in-laws to determine when they are invited to my house.
- From now on I [will not] entertain my in-laws when they drop by unexpectedly.
- From now on [I will] allow my in-laws to invite themselves over [once a month].
- From now on [I will] entertain my in-laws when they drop by unexpectedly as long as it is [before 8 PM].

Now write your own boundary statements.

#3 *They beg us to come visit them all the time...especially during the holidays.*

It's the day after Thanksgiving and you're glad to be back at your own house after having spent the entire weekend visiting your in-laws. *At least I won't have to go visit them again any time soon,* you think to yourself. Wrong! The phone rings and you know instantly who it is and what they want before your husband even answers the call. You run to hide in the coat closet but there's no escape. You overhear your husband agreeing to go to his parents' house for every holiday between now and the time you die.

Here are some things to consider when setting boundaries about visiting your in-laws. Avoid routine visits that occur every week on a certain day. Keep your visits irregular so you have the freedom to decide each week whether you want to visit them or do something different. It's also important to realize your in-laws feel dominant in their own house because that's their territory. If your goal is to achieve equal footing with them, consider meeting at your house or a neutral location instead. Remember, you don't have to visit your in-laws just because your husband wants to see them; sometimes he can visit them without you.

WHAT DO *YOU* THINK?

1. Do you prefer to talk on the phone, e-mail, write letters, or go visit your in-laws? _____

2. Do your in-laws invite you to come visit more often than you'd like to visit? Yes No

3. **With your schedule and needs in mind, how often would you like to visit your in-laws?**
    _____ 2-3 times a week   _____ Once a week
    _____ Every other week   _____ Once a month
    _____ Every other month   _____ Other

4. How long would you prefer visits with your in-laws to be?
    _____ Less than 3 hours   _____ One day
    _____ 2-3 days   _____ 4-6 days

5. Where and with whom would you like to spend the following holidays this year?
    Mother's Day?_____ Your birthday?_____
    Christmas?_____ Other?_____

EXAMPLES OF BOUNDARY STATEMENTS:

- From now on, I [will not] visit my in-laws out of guilt.
- From now on, I am willing to visit my in-laws [once per month]³.
- From now on, I am willing to visit my in-laws at their house [1-2 times per year].
- From now on, I am willing to visit my in-laws for no longer than [3 days] at a time.
- From now on, I am no longer willing to spend [every Sunday afternoon] at my in-laws' house even though that is the expected tradition.
- This year I am willing to spend [Thanksgiving] at my in-laws' house, but I'm not willing to spend [Christmas] with them⁴.

Now write your own boundary statements.

---

³ How often you visit your in-laws will depend on how close you live to them, your work schedule, etc.

⁴ It's important to negotiate a fair compromise with your husband before setting boundaries about holidays with your in-laws. We'll look at how to do that in the second half of this book.

#4 *They give unwanted advice and meddle in things that aren't their business.*

It's a nice, sunny Saturday and you are preparing yourself mentally to spend the afternoon at the mall with your mother-in-law. "This music is awful," she complains as she changes the radio station in *your* car. An hour later you are standing in line to buy a pretty, white blouse when she says, "You should wear more vibrant blouses so you won't look so pale all of the time." You restrain yourself from strangling her with the hanger and tell her it's time to head back home so you can watch your favorite soap opera. She lets out a deep sigh of disapproval and urges you to sell your TV so you can spend your free time doing more important things such as helping out at the orphanage or hosting a telethon for the mentally disabled.

Disrespectful people give advice by implying you are a moron or a sinner if you don't behave the way they think you should. To seek or accept advice from these people is usually a bad idea because to do so would encourage them to treat you as inferior.

WHAT DO *YOU* THINK?

1. Name some specific things your in-laws give you advice about.
    (For example: child rearing, finances, diet, clothes, music, job,
    education, purchases, home decor, etc.)

    _____

2. How does it make you feel when they give you advice about these
    things? _____

3. Would you prefer it if they didn't give you advice about these
    things? Yes No

4. Are you willing to hear their advice about any topics? Yes No
    If yes, then which topics?

    _____

5. What resources do you turn to when you want advice about
    something? (For example: Consumer Reports, books, friends,
    professionals, your husband, your own parents, etc.)

    _____

EXAMPLES OF BOUNDARY STATEMENTS:

- From now on, whenever my in-laws give me advice about [how
  we spend our money or how we spend our time], I will discourage
  them from doing it again in the future.
- From now on, whenever my in-laws give me advice in an
  intrusive, controlling or condescending manner, I will [discourage
  them from doing it again in the future].
- From now on, I will listen to (but not necessarily follow) my in-
  laws' advice about [recipes or cleaning products] as long as they
  offer it in a respectful, unobtrusive manner.

Now write your own boundary statements.

#5 They control us with money.

"Nice car!" your friend says as you pull up in your new red convertible, "I bet that cost a pretty penny." You aren't sure how to respond. On one hand, the car has cost you nothing because your in-laws are making the payments for you. On the other hand, the car has cost you everything -- your freedom, pride, and independence. Your in-laws think that because they are making the payments, they have the right to control all of your financial decisions. You feel trapped but it's hard to break free because you work for your father-in-law, your mother-in-law provides free daycare, and you live in their house. You don't know how to dig your way out of this mess and every time you try, your in-laws accuse you of being ungrateful for their generosity.

Here are a couple of things to consider while setting boundaries on this issue. You have a right to be in control of your own finances, in fact you have a *responsibility* to be in control of your own finances. You aren't an ungrateful person if you decide you want to move to a less expensive house, get a less expensive car, change jobs, or change babysitters so you aren't in a position for your in-laws to control you with money.

You may thoroughly enjoy the fact that your in-laws are providing a nice home, car, education, childcare, and/or job for you and you don't want to take steps to become financially independent from them. If that's the case, then you must realize your behavior is encouraging them to control you with money. If you want your in-laws to stop interfering with your financial decisions, then you must stop accepting their help. You can't have it both ways.

WHAT DO *YOU* THINK?

1. Have your in-laws helped you purchase things in the past? If so, what (for example, a house, car, education, etc.)?
   _____

2. Are your in-laws currently helping you pay for anything? If so, what? _____

3. Do your in-laws try to influence your daily financial decisions because they feel they have earned the right to do so? Yes   No

4. What are your in-laws currently paying for that you'd rather be in charge of yourself? (For example: house, car, education, childcare, job, credit card, groceries)_____

5. What are you willing to do to become financially independent? (For example: do without some things or pick up some overtime pay at work)_____

EXAMPLES OF BOUNDARY STATEMENTS:

- I am no longer willing to let my in-laws control me; therefore I will be solely responsible for [my car payment] instead of accepting financial help from them.

- I am no longer willing to let my in-laws control me financially; therefore I will [pick up a temporary job over the holidays] in order to [pay back the money they loaned us].

Now write your own boundary statements.

#6 They make hurtful comments and then say they're only teasing.

You and your husband have invited his parents over to your house for dinner. Everything seems to be going fine until you offer your father-in-law a second portion of lasagna and he scoffs, "No, thanks. The first helping was torture enough." You're embarrassed and angry; you don't know whether to cry or scream. You look to your husband in hopes that he will demand an apology from his dad. But much to your horror, your husband is laughing too! Somehow you manage to be civil throughout the rest of the evening but as soon as they leave, you corner your husband and say, "Your dad is an insensitive jerk. How dare you laugh while he verbally abuses me! It would've been nice if you had defended me." Your husband accuses you of being too sensitive and suggests you lighten up.

Here are some things to consider when setting boundaries on this issue. You don't need to pretend you enjoy your in-laws' sarcastic sense of humor. And just because you don't find it hilarious when your in-laws tease you unmercifully doesn't mean you have a lousy sense of humor.

WHAT DO *YOU* THINK?

1. Do your in-laws make comments that you find hurtful? Yes   No
2. Does it happen often enough that you feel the problem needs to be addressed? Yes   No
3. Do your in-laws make a habit of teasing everyone, or just you?
4. Do you and your in-laws have a similar sense of humor? Yes   No
5. Do your in-laws think it's funny when other people tease them? Yes   No

6. Does it tend to irritate you more when your in-laws tease you about something than when your friends tease you about the same thing? Yes   No   If so, why do you think that is? _____

7. What are some things you don't like to be teased about?
   _____

8. Do YOU (not your in-laws or your husband) think you may be too sensitive about any of these things? Yes   No

9. Have you ever told your in-laws they hurt your feelings when they make certain comments? Yes   No   If so, how did they respond?

10. Do you feel that they responded appropriately? Yes   No

11. If someone were to tell you they were hurt by a comment you made, how would you respond? _____

12. Put a checkmark next to the responses you think are appropriate when someone tells you that you have hurt their feelings.
    _____ "You're too sensitive."
    _____ "I was just kidding."
    _____ "I'm sorry. I didn't mean to hurt your feelings."
    _____ "You have no sense of humor."
    _____ "We have a different sense of humor."

> It's okay to feel sad, hurt, angry, and/or embarrassed when someone says something hurtful to you. If someone tells you that you shouldn't have these feelings, then they are violating your right to have feelings. That having been said, it's also very important to be able to laugh at yourself. If you find that you are constantly offended by a lot of different people, then perhaps you should take an honest look at yourself to see if you need to stop taking things so personally. I challenge you to find a balance between learning to shrug things off versus confidently protecting yourself against verbally abusive people.

EXAMPLES OF BOUNDARY STATEMENTS:

- From now on, I will try not to let it bug me so much when my in-laws make comments about [my chicken casserole, my purple corduroy pants, and my inability to return a rented movie on time].
- From now on, I am no longer willing to be teased about [my weight or the way I raise my kids].

Now write your own boundary statements.

#7 *They manipulate me with hidden messages and nonverbal communication.*

It's Easter morning and you have just arrived at your in-laws' house for breakfast. Instead of greeting you with a warm hello, your mother-in-law raises an eyebrow to let you know she thinks you are dressed like a whore. You find yourself wanting to apologize for committing a sin, but then you realize your outfit is perfectly decent and that your mother-in-law has never worn anything but a turtleneck. You're tempted to turn to your husband for sympathy but you don't because you know he'll say he didn't hear his mom say anything bad about your dress...and technically she didn't. She doesn't need words to manipulate you; all she needs is an eyebrow.

Here are a couple of things to consider when setting boundaries on this issue. You don't have to let your in-laws manipulate you with a sigh, disapproving glance, or certain tone of voice. You are capable of determining when you are being manipulated regardless of whether or not your in-laws (or your husband) admit what is really going on.

WHAT DO *YOU* THINK?

1. Do you ever get the feeling your in-laws are manipulating you but you can't pinpoint what they said or did to make you feel that way? Yes No

2. Do you ever feel ashamed of your opinions, clothes, etc. after your in-laws give you a look of disapproval? Yes   No
3. Do you often behave the way your mother-in-law wants you to behave in order to avoid hearing a deep sigh of disappointment from her? Yes   No
4. Do you ever slip into the role of an apologetic, frightened child after your in-laws use a certain tone of voice with you? Yes   No
5. Do your in-laws say subtle things to make *you* look bad and *them* look good? Yes No
6. Do you ever get the feeling your in-laws are insulting you by *saying* one thing but *meaning* something else? Yes   No
7. Do you find that you want to confront your in-laws about manipulating you, but you can't figure out how to do that because they aren't manipulating you in an obvious way? Yes No
8. Do you find yourself trying to convince your husband that your in-laws are manipulative but then you can't figure out how to prove it? Yes No

EXAMPLES OF BOUNDARY STATEMENTS:

- From now on, I [am not] willing to let my in-laws manipulate me with hidden messages and nonverbal communication.
- From now on, I will [confront my in-laws] whenever they manipulate me by [shaking their head with disapproval, sighing in disgust, or lifting an eyebrow].

Now write your own boundary statements.

#8 They expect me to call them "Mom" and "Dad."

It's the night of your engagement and your soon-to-be husband excitedly tells his parents the great news. His mom throws her arms around you and in between all her blubbering, she manages to say, "You're family now, so call us "Mom" and "Dad" from now on!"

Some women call their in-laws "Mom" and "Dad" and it isn't a problem for them. However, if you are a woman whose in-laws treat you as inferior (and I assume you are because you're reading this book) then you may be adding to the problem by addressing them in a way that encourages them to feel superior to you. If you are currently calling your in-laws "Mom" and "Dad" (or "Mr." and "Mrs."), that could be part of the reason they don't respect your needs as an adult. Call them by their first names if they call you by your first name... this will communicate you are on an equal level with them. You aren't disrespecting them by calling them by their first names any more than they are disrespecting you by calling you by your first name.

WHAT DO *YOU* THINK?

1. Do you feel uncomfortable calling your in-laws "Mom" and "Dad"? Yes No

2. Do you feel obligated to call your in-laws "Mom" and "Dad" because that's what they prefer? Yes   No
3. Do you call them "Mom" and "Dad" because you feel it would be disrespectful to do otherwise? Yes   No
4. Do you call them "Mom" and "Dad" because you don't want to upset them (or your husband)? Yes   No
5. Do you currently call your in-laws "Mr." and "Mrs."? Yes   No
6. Would you prefer to call your in-laws by their first names? Yes   No
7. Do you feel offended when your in-laws call you by your first name? Yes   No

EXAMPLES OF BOUNDARY STATEMENTS:

- From now on, I [will not] call my in-laws "Mom" and "Dad."
- From now on, I will call my in-laws [Helen] and [Harry].

Now write your own boundary statements.

#9 My mother-in-law expects me to be the daughter she never had.

"Would you like to go out to lunch with me today?" your mother-in-law asks in a hopeful voice. It's your only day off and the last thing you want to do is spend it with her but you don't want to disappoint her and so you say yes. Her excitement is matched only by that of your husband; he has long hoped you and his mom would become best friends. After lunch, your mother-in-law suggests going to a movie. After the movie she invites you to the mall. Eventually you come up with an excuse to go home but, as you wave goodbye, she asks what you are doing the next day. *I'm going to move and not tell you my new address,* you think to yourself.

> If you have a mother-in-law who treats you as an equal adult and respects your opinions, wants, and needs, then you may have a sincere desire to have a close relationship with her. However, if you have a mother-in-law who talks down to you and thinks her opinions, wants, and needs are superior to yours, then you're no more likely to desire a close relationship with her than with Satan. If you don't want to have a close relationship with your mother-in-law, there's probably a good reason[5].

WHAT DO *YOU* THINK?

1. Do you enjoy spending time with your mother-in-law? Yes No
2. Do you and your mother-in-law share similar interests or hobbies? Yes No
3. Do you feel good about yourself when you are with her? Yes No
4. Does your mother-in-law respect your opinions, wants, and needs? Yes No
5. Do you view your mother-in-law as a friend or a "parent"?

   _____
6. Does she treat you as a friend or a child? _____

---

[5] It's common for a mother-in-law with no daughters to look to their daughter-in-law to fill that void. But if that daughter-in-law already has a close relationship with her own mom, then she probably won't have a strong desire to have a really close relationship with her mother-in-law. These different expectations can cause tension and hurt feelings.

7. Does your mother-in-law want to have a closer relationship with you than you want with her? Yes   No
8. Do you feel obligated to have a close relationship just because she wants one? Yes   No
9. Do you feel obligated to have a close relationship with her just because that's what your husband wants? Yes   No
10. How often does your mother-in-law want to talk to you on the phone?_____
11. How often do you want to talk to her on the phone?
    _____
12. How often does your mother-in-law want to go on outings with you? _____
13. How often do you want to go on outings with her?

    _____

EXAMPLES OF BOUNDARY STATEMENTS:

- From now on, I will talk to my mother-in-law on the phone [when I want to (about once a week)] instead of [when she wants me to (every day)].
- From now on, I will go on outings with her [when I want to (once a month)] instead of [when she wants me to (once a week)].

Now write your own boundary statements.

#10 My mother-in-law gossips about me to my husband, friends, and other family members.[6]

You and your husband get into the car to head home after a visit with his parents. As you think back over the day, you congratulate yourself for making such a gallant effort to get along with them. There had been several times when you felt the urge to throw things at your in-laws, but you kept your composure. But then to your amazement, your husband glares at you and says, "I can't believe you were so mean to my parents today!" You are completely shocked. "What do you mean?" you say, "I went out of my way to be nice to them." He explains that his mother complained to him that you were rude to her. "I want you to call and apologize to her," he demanded. You can't figure out who you're angrier with, your mother-in-law for trying to turn your own husband against you, or your husband for letting her succeed.

Consider the following when setting boundaries on this issue. When your in-laws try to influence your husband to view you in a negative way, that is a major threat to your marriage. This is totally unacceptable behavior on their part and you need to do everything in your power to put an end to it. It may be tough to pinpoint exactly what they are saying that is negative about you because they may be subtle. For instance they may tell your husband, "We go out of our way to do things for your wife but we can't figure out how to get her to like us." This subtle criticism is

---

[6] I realize that your father-in-law may also gossip about you...and that's not okay either.

gossip because it gives your husband the impression that his parents are the good guys and that you are the bad guy. A statement like that causes him to feel as though his parents are victims, and he may try to come to their defense by assuming the worst about you. Pay careful attention to the subtle messages your in-laws may be sending to your husband.

WHAT DO *YOU* THINK?

1. Do you know or suspect that your mother-in-law gossips about you to your husband, friends, and/or other family members?
   Yes No
2. Does your mother-in-law gossip *to you* about other people?
   Yes No
3. Does your husband often misjudge you because of something his mom told him instead of giving you the benefit of the doubt?
   Yes No
4. Does your husband seem to be more critical of you after he has spent time with his mom? Yes No
5. How do you usually react when you find out your mother-in-law has gossiped about you to others?

   _____

6. What would you like for your husband, friends, and other family members to say or do the next time your mother-in-law starts to say something negative about you? _____

EXAMPLES OF BOUNDARY STATEMENTS:

- From now on I [will] do something to try to minimize the effect of my mother-in-law's gossip.

Now write your own boundary statements.

In the beginning of this chapter, I asked you to make a list of things your in-laws do that make you feel upset. If there are things on your list that I have not addressed in this chapter, take time now to stop and write boundaries[7].

I hope you learned some important things about your opinions and needs in this chapter. Now that you have set some boundaries, it's time to learn how to enforce them.

---

[7] See the chapter entitled "How Many Forms of Birth Control Can We Safely Use at the Same Time?" to learn how to deal with in-laws who interfere with raising your children. See the chapter called "Help! I've Fallen...Could You Bring Me My Roller Blades?" to learn how to deal with elderly in-laws who act more helpless than they are and expect you to take care of their every need.

Chapter 4

Don't Stand So Close to Me
Learning how to enforce boundaries with your in-laws

Insanity is doing the same thing over and over again and expecting different results.
--Albert Einstein

Imagine if you woke up one morning and decided to paint your living room blue. You go through the whole process of buying supplies, prepping the room, and putting on a coat of primer. Then you painstakingly apply two coats of the shade you chose: Rain Mist Blue. Hours later you clean all of your brushes and paint rollers and then stand back to admire your work. And that's when you realize you don't like the way Rain Mist Blue looks in your living room. So you decide to paint the room again the next day in hopes of achieving the desired look. You go through the entire ordeal again…but when you are finished you still don't like the way the paint looks. That's because you painted the room Rain Mist Blue again instead of trying a different shade. "Tomorrow I'll try painting the room Rain Mist Blue for the third time," you tell yourself, "maybe I'll like it then." Sounds crazy, doesn't it?

When you behave a certain way and don't get the results you want, then it makes sense to change your behavior instead of doing the same thing over and over again. Whether you are painting a room or interacting with difficult in-laws, if your past behavior hasn't achieved the desired results, then you need to try something else. In the last chapter I prepared you to come up with new behavior patterns by helping you determine some boundaries based on your needs. Now it's time to communicate and enforce those boundaries with your in-laws. This chapter will give you ideas on how to do that in a dignified manner.

#1 *They call too early, too late, and too often.*

Go back and look at the boundary statements you made on this issue in the previous chapter. In those statements, you addressed the following issues: (1) what time of day/night you don't want to talk on the phone, (2) which activities you prefer not to have interrupted by phone calls, (3) which way(s) you prefer to communicate with your in-laws, and (4) how often you'd like to communicate with them.

Enforcing boundaries involves communicating your needs to people in hope that they will modify their behavior, but it's important to remember that enforcing boundaries involves a change in *your* behavior, not theirs. When you ask someone to respect your needs, be ready to change your behavior in order to make sure your boundary is respected whether or not they change their behavior. For instance, if you ask your in-laws to stop calling after 9PM and they stop calling after 9PM, that's great. But if they continue to call after 9PM, you must change your behavior (for example, you could turn the ringer off at 9PM) since they didn't change their behavior; otherwise you haven't enforced a boundary.

There are many different things you can SAY and/or DO to communicate and enforce your boundaries. I will give you several ideas so you can decide which might be the best solution for you. Don't be afraid to try several different approaches until you find one that works. Feel free to be creative and brainstorm your own solutions. As you read through these suggestions of things to say and do, put an 'X' beside an approach you'd like to try.

Here are some things you can SAY to communicate your boundaries about phone calls:

_____ "Feel free to call as early in the morning as you want, but I'd appreciate it if you would make your evening calls before 8PM since we go to bed early."

_____ "I know you're excited to talk to us, but we love to sleep in on Saturdays and I'd sure appreciate it if you would make your calls after 10AM."

_____ "It's easier for me to talk to you in the evenings instead of the mornings because then I'm not rushing to get ready for work."

_____ "You deserve to have my undivided attention on the phone, so from now on if you call while I'm [putting the kids in bed / cooking dinner] I will call you back later. I want you to feel free to do the same to me if I call you at an inconvenient time."

_____ "You and I can still have a close relationship even if we don't talk every day."

Here are some things you can DO to enforce your boundaries about phone calls:

_____ Get Caller ID and/or an answering machine and screen their calls[1]. (Besides maxi pads with wings, Caller ID is the best invention ever.)

_____ Don't return your in-laws' call right away. Wait until the next day. Then the next time they call, wait two days before calling them back. Continue in this manner until you have established a communication pattern of your choice (once per week) instead of theirs (every day).

_____ Don't always return their call with another call if you prefer a different form of communication. Respond to the message they left on your answering machine by sending them a short e-mail. Or drop a quick note in the mail. Or talk to them the next time you see them in person.

_____ Turn your ringer off at a certain time of night.

_____ Change your number and don't give them the new one[2].

Although you may need harsher boundaries with your in-laws than you do with your friends or your own parents, it may be a good idea to maintain some consistency with everyone in order to gain your husband's loyalty. If you choose to screen all calls (not just those from his parents) during dinner, then your husband won't think you're just picking on his parents to be mean.

---

[1] If you want to have some fun, you can record the country song 'Here's a quarter, call someone who cares' as your outgoing message.
[2] I'm mostly kidding about this one too, but wouldn't it be fun?

#2 They invite themselves over and drop by unannounced.

Take a look back at the boundary statements you made on this issue in the previous chapter. In those statements, you addressed the following issues: (1) whether or not you will allow your in-laws to determine when they are invited to your house and, if so, how often it is okay for them to invite themselves over and (2) whether or not you will entertain your in-laws when they drop by unexpectedly and, if so, are there any days/times that you do you *not* want them to drop by.

Here are some things you can SAY if your in-laws invite themselves over or drop by unannounced[3]:

_____ "Now is not a good time for me. How about coming Wednesday instead and then I'll be able to give you my undivided attention?"

_____ "This isn't a convenient time for me to visit with you. It would be great if you could call first before dropping by. That way I can let you know whether or not I'm available so you don't waste a trip."

_____ "I love it when you come by to visit but [Fridays / mornings / the dinner hour] isn't a convenient time for me to have visitors. Feel free to come any other time."

_____ "I'll think about that and get back to you." (This is my favorite way to respond when people invite themselves to my house because it's easy to remember and it buys me time to think about what I really want and how to communicate that to them in a respectful manner. Sometimes I reply to them by e-mail so they can't pressure me over the phone.)

_____ "We're looking forward to your visit next month, but it isn't going to work for us to have you here for two weeks. You're welcome to come stay with us Friday through Sunday, but if you decide to stay in town after Sunday then we need for you to stay at a hotel."[4]

---

[3] Try to avoid giving specific excuses because that may backfire. For example, if you say, "I can't invite you in because I'm on my way to the grocery store," they might say, "We need groceries too. We'll come with you." The more vague you are, the less likely you are to be cornered.

[4] For more suggestions on how you and/or your husband can ask his parents to stay in a hotel, see chapter 25 of I'm OK, You're My Parents by Dale Atkins, Ph.D.

> If your in-laws invite themselves on an outing with you (instead of to your house), then you can say something like this: "Tonight isn't a good time for you to come with us to the movie since it's a date. Let's plan on all of us going to a movie together next weekend if you're available then."

Here are some things you can DO to discourage your in-laws from inviting themselves over and dropping by unannounced:

_____ Be the one to initiate invitations to your in-laws so they don't feel the need to invite themselves. For example, if Easter is coming up and you know they'll probably call and invite themselves over, call and invite them first. Be sure to let them know specifically which days they are invited so they leave when you want them to leave instead of giving them the chance to decide to stay longer than they are welcome.

_____ Try to anticipate when your in-laws are likely to invite themselves over and make alternate plans ahead of time. For example, if your in-laws usually drop by after their synchronized swimming class on Monday mornings, then start planning trips to the grocery store during that time. (If you find you are constantly inconveniencing yourself in order to avoid them, then you may need to try a different approach.) Another example would be to make early plans for the holidays so when they invite themselves to your house for Christmas, you can say you've already decided to go to your brother's house. By having a plan in advance you'll have more control over visiting patterns without having to lie, throw up, or kill anyone.

_____ Don't answer the door. You aren't being any more rude by not answering the door than they are by showing up without an invitation. If they ask you later why you didn't answer the door, be honest and tell them you weren't up to having company. (If you just make up some false excuse, they won't get the message that you don't want them to show up uninvited and you'll just prolong the agony for everyone.)

_____ Answer the door and let them know they can come in for a few minutes but then you have some things you need to do. When you're ready for them to go, thank them for coming and escort them to the door.

_____ Answer the door but don't invite them in. Tell them you're not up to having company right now. If this method doesn't work because they're about to barge in past you, remember you can always fake death like possums do.

_____ Change the locks on your doors if they let themselves in when you don't want them to. Don't give them the new key[5]. If they say their key isn't working anymore, just say nonchalantly you had the locks changed.

_____ Consider moving away from your in-laws if it will help your marriage[6]. Here's how to tell if you live too close to your in-laws. Get a map of the United States and condense it until it fits onto a 3" x 5" index card. Put your finger down where you live. Put another finger down where they live. If your fingers touch, then you need to move farther away. Your spouse may be reluctant to agree to this solution, but don't worry. Just rent a big truck, pack up your belongings and tell him you're just taking him for a drive. Chances are he won't even notice that you moved. If he's anything like my husband, he's only thinking about sex[7].

---

[5] Duh.

[6] If you're wondering if the Witness Protection Program will help you, they won't. I know; I've asked.

[7] Joking aside, I will give you suggestions on how to approach your spouse about moving farther away from his parents in the chapter called "I Am Rubber, You Are Glue."

Be careful about offering your master bedroom to your in-laws when they come to visit. Although offering guests your bedroom is a kind gesture, your in-laws may *expect* their "kids" to give up their room. Instead of being thankful for your generosity, they may feel you *owe* them your master bedroom because they are superior to you. Obviously you don't want to encourage that. Evaluate the attitude of your in-laws. If they seem to be unassuming and sincerely appreciative, then go ahead and offer them your room if that's what you want to do. But if you experience power struggles with your in-laws and you sense a lack of respect from them, then seize every opportunity available to claim your equal status with them. By offering them the guest room, the hide-a-bed in the living room, or even a rental bed, you are communicating that you call the shots at your house, not them. If they don't like their choices, then offer to call and check on some hotel prices for them. After all, do they offer you their room when you visit them? Probably not. So why should you feel guilty if you do the same thing? It's your house. Whatever you decide, remember that you don't need their approval to determine 'rules' for your own household.

#3 *They beg <u>us</u> to come visit <u>them</u> all the time . . . especially during the holidays.*

Take a look back at the boundary statements you made on this issue in the previous chapter. In those statements, you addressed the following issues: (1) how often you are willing to visit your in-laws[8], (2) how long you'd like for those visits to last, and (3) where and with whom you are (or are not) willing to spend holidays this year.

Here are some things you can SAY to communicate your boundaries about visits[9]:

_____ "I can't make it this time, but thanks for the invitation."

_____ "Thanks for the invitation. I'll think about that and get back to you." (Make sure you really do get back to them via telephone or e-mail, etc.)

_____ "I can't visit you on Saturday, but I could come Monday instead if that works for you."

_____ "I'll plan on coming by with the kids on Saturday for a visit, but we'll need to leave by 3PM."

_____ "We enjoy getting together with you for brunch on Sundays, but instead of meeting at your house every week, let's vary the time and place. Are you available to go to dinner with us at Red Lobster on Friday the 5th?" (If the visit is at your own house or a restaurant, consider inviting friends, neighbors, co-workers, or siblings to spice up the old routine.)

_____ "We can come out to see you in June, but we've decided to stay for three days instead of the whole week." (Make sure whenever you say "we" that you have reached a compromise with your husband first.)

_____ "We'll spend Friday and Saturday with you, and then we'll spend Sunday with friends."

_____ "We'll plan on coming out to see you during our vacation, but we will stay in a hotel."

_____ "We can come out and see you for Christmas Eve, but we will be spending Christmas Day at our own house."

---

[8] You may choose to make an exception every now and then in order to show you love your husband, thus moving you closer to your goal of gaining his loyalty.

[9] You'll probably be more likely to gain your husband's loyalty if you change the details of a visit instead of declining the whole invitation.

_____ "We're not going to be able to make it to your house for
Christmas this year, but thank you for the invitation."[10]

_____ "We'd like to spend Thanksgiving with you, but we'd like to
have it at our house this year. We hope you can come." (This is a
great solution if you can't afford travel expenses or you don't feel
like figuring out who's going to take care of your pet piranhas
while you're away.)

_____ "Thanks for inviting us, but we're going to be spending Easter
with my aunt."

> You can only decline an invitation that is directed toward you. If
> your husband is being invited, then let him make his own decision as to
> whether or not he wants to go. He will resent you if you make his
> decisions for him and you may decrease your chances of gaining his
> loyalty.

Here are some things you can DO to enforce your boundaries about
visits:

_____ Anticipate when your in-laws will ask you to come visit and
schedule things in advance before they invite you. (Tell your
husband in March that you want to spend Christmas with your
aunt in Florida.)

_____ If you do decide to visit your in-laws, schedule things
throughout the visit that will give you a break from having to
interact with them constantly. Suggest inviting a family friend(s)
over to play games, go for a walk by yourself, see a movie, take a
nap, go with your husband to see his old high school buddy, or
call a good friend just to chat. For more freedom, stay in a hotel
and get a rental car.

_____ If you decide to go visit your in-laws but you don't want to visit
as long as your husband wants to visit. . . spend a day or two at
your in-laws' house and then leave. You can meet up with your
husband at home.

---

[10] If they continue to pester you, tell them, "We have converted to Islam and will no
longer be celebrating Christmas" or "My boss has given me a temporary work
assignment in Czechoslovakia over the holidays."

_____ Instead of feeling obligated to follow your in-laws' traditions, think of new traditions. Suggest serving Thanksgiving dinner to homeless people or go on a Christmas cruise with your in-laws, friends, and/or your own parents.

_____ Try to reach a compromise that will meet the needs of your husband, his parents, and yourself without becoming an obsessive people pleaser. For example, if your husband wants to spend Christmas vacation with his parents, but you really wanted to go skiing instead, consider spending Christmas Day with his parents and then leave and spend the rest of the vacation skiing with your hubby.

#4 *They give unwanted advice and meddle in things that aren't their business.*

Take a look back at the boundary statements you made on this issue in the previous chapter. In those statements, you addressed the following issues: (1) which topics you are—and are not—willing to receive advice about from your in-laws and (2) what you consider to be an acceptable (and unacceptable) manner for your in-laws to give you advice.

Here are some things you can SAY to communicate your boundaries about advice and meddling:

_____ "It looks like we'll have to agree to disagree."

_____ "You're entitled to your opinion."[11]

_____ "I realize you don't approve of how I spend my money but this is my decision."

_____ "I know you're probably just trying to protect me from making a poor decision, but I need you to accept the fact that I may make some poor decisions sometimes, as everyone does, and I will assume responsibility for those decisions."

_____ "I know you're probably just trying to help but I would be more receptive to your advice if you waited until I asked for it."

_____ "I appreciate your input, but when you use that tone of voice, I feel as if I'm being judged and talked down to. From now on when you want to share your opinion with me, I need for you to talk to me as you would a friend and then leave the decision to me."

_____ "Why do you ask?"[12]

_____ "I'd rather not say."

_____ "I know you're probably just trying to help, but this is between my husband and me."[13]

_____ "From now on I need for you to stop going through my mail and eavesdropping on my phone conversations."

---

[11] This indicates that you respect their difference of opinion but that you aren't going to let their difference of opinion bother you.

[12] This is a good response if they ask how much you paid for your new car and you don't want to tell them.

[13] This is a good response if, for example, they ask what you and your husband were fighting about the night before.

Here are some things you can DO to enforce your boundaries about advice and meddling:

_____ Avoid talking to your in-laws about things you don't want them to give you advice about. For instance, if it drives you crazy when your in-laws make comments about your spending, then don't tell them how much money you make, what you spend your money on, how much you paid for your big screen TV, etc.

_____ Avoid putting yourself in a position that invites their unwanted advice and/or meddling. For instance, if you hate it when your in-laws criticize your driving, let someone else drive when they are in the car.

#5 *They control us with money.*

Take a look back at the boundary statements you made on this issue in the previous chapter. In those statements, you addressed the following issues: (1) which things you will stop letting your in-laws pay for and (2) what you are willing to do in order to gain financial independence.

Here are some things you can SAY to communicate your boundaries about finances:

_____ "Thank you for helping us out with our (car, house, etc.) payments. I'm excited to say we will be able to make those payments by ourselves from now on."

_____ "Here is the money we owe you. Thank you so much for loaning it to us."

_____ "I've made some changes in our finances and I've decided to start taking more responsibility for childcare. Our kids really enjoy being with you and I'd still love for you to baby-sit every now and then when it's convenient for you, but I don't need for you to watch them every day anymore. Thanks for taking such good care of our kids."

_____ "We've decided to start taking more responsibility for our finances. We are so thankful for your offer to help us get a nicer [car] than we could afford on our own, but we've decided to get one that's within our budget instead. Thanks again for your generosity."[14]

I once saw a movie where a father's advice to his daughter was "Make more or desire less."[15] What a great way to achieve financial independence!

---

[14] Stating boundaries about money is tricky if you and your husband aren't in agreement. Later in the book we'll look at how to gain your husband's loyalty... but in the meantime, remember that your boundary statements are about what you alone can enforce, whether or not you have your hubby's support.

[15] *Comfort and Joy (2003)*

Here are some things you can DO to enforce your boundaries about finances:

_____ Establish and follow a budget to help you live within your means. If necessary, cancel cable TV, do without your weekly manicure and/or pack a lunch instead of eating out.

_____ Stop going on shopping trips. Leave your credit cards at home. Discipline yourself not to buy something if you can't afford to pay cash for it. Save up for purchases in advance.

_____ See a financial advisor who can help you implement a plan to become financially independent. He/she may advise you to pay back your high interest car loan (or credit card debt) by taking out a low interest home equity loan. Or he/she may advise you on how to plan for your child's education.

_____ Find a different job with a higher salary. (If you feel like you aren't in charge of your own finances because you work for your in-laws, find a different job.)

_____ Work extra hours (at the job you have now or at a temporary second job) in order to pay back the money you owe your in-laws.

_____ Have a garage sale and use the money toward what you owe your in-laws.

_____ Take out a loan from a bank to pay your in-laws what you owe them.

_____ Sell your house and move to a less expensive one.

_____ Find alternate childcare besides your in-laws. Hire a babysitter, find a daycare, or stay home with the kids instead. (You might be surprised to find that you can save money by staying home with the kids yourself rather than paying for daycare).

_____ Move out of their house if you are living with them now. Often couples decide to live at a parent's house while they save up for their own house. Buying a house is usually a fantastic investment, but you may want to consider postponing or even foregoing your purchase if a strong marriage is more important to you. Consider living in an apartment for a few extra years instead of having your marriage destroyed by the stress of living with your in-laws.

_____ Show your in-laws you are financially independent by paying for your own meals when you go out to restaurants. If they insist on paying for your meal, then insist on paying for theirs the next time you go out together.

61

If you are currently borrowing money from your in-laws, then it may be fine to continue doing so if (1) you don't feel obligated to have your in-laws approve of every thing you spend money on and (2) they don't try to control your financial decisions. Even when borrowing from family, it's very important to put the loan in writing and agree on a payment schedule and interest rate. The more professional you keep the transaction, the better chance of avoiding problems in the future.

#6 *They make hurtful comments and then say they're only teasing.*

Take a look back at the boundary statements you made on this issue in the previous chapter. In those statements, you addressed the following issues: (1) which things you *will* allow your in-laws to tease you about and (2) which things you *will not* allow your in-laws to tease you about.

Here are some things you can SAY when your in-laws tease you about something that you are *not* willing to let them tease you about:

_____ "When you made that comment about [the way I clean my house] I felt like you were criticizing me. Was that your intention?" (It's possible that your in-laws don't realize they are hurting your feelings. By confronting them about it, you are giving them the chance to learn what hurts your feelings and to apologize for hurting you.)

_____ "I know you're probably not doing it intentionally, but it hurts my feelings when you tease me about [my cooking]."

_____ "I know you love to tease each other, but I didn't grow up in a sarcastic family, so when you tease me it comes across to me as a personal attack. Neither of us is wrong; we just have a different sense of humor. I need for you to stop teasing me about [the way I raise my kids] and in exchange I'll try to take it less personally if sometimes you forget."

_____ "I'd like to have a better relationship with you and in order for that to happen, I need for you to stop making hurtful comments to me about [my weight]."

_____ "I've asked you before not to criticize me about [my nose]. The next time you do so, I will leave the conversation (by hanging up the phone or leaving the premises)."

Here are some things you can DO when your in-laws tease you about something you are *not* willing to let them tease you about:

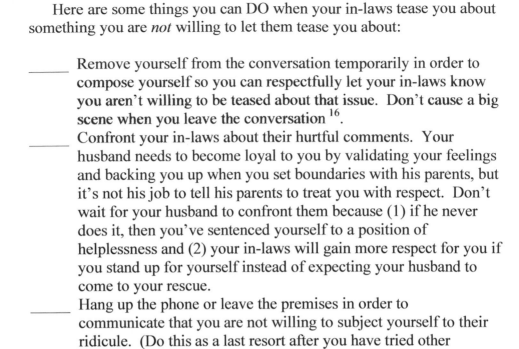

_____ Remove yourself from the conversation temporarily in order to compose yourself so you can respectfully let your in-laws know you aren't willing to be teased about that issue. Don't cause a big scene when you leave the conversation [16].

_____ Confront your in-laws about their hurtful comments. Your husband needs to become loyal to you by validating your feelings and backing you up when you set boundaries with his parents, but it's not his job to tell his parents to treat you with respect. Don't wait for your husband to confront them because (1) if he never does it, then you've sentenced yourself to a position of helplessness and (2) your in-laws will gain more respect for you if you stand up for yourself instead of expecting your husband to come to your rescue.

_____ Hang up the phone or leave the premises in order to communicate that you are not willing to subject yourself to their ridicule. (Do this as a last resort after you have tried other solutions first.)

If your in-laws choose to continually make hurtful comments despite your assertive attempts to get them to stop, then you need to protect your self-esteem from the negative effects of their verbal abuse. You can (1) limit the amount of time you spend with them in order to prevent *their* opinion of you from affecting *your* opinion of you and (2) bring an encouraging friend along on visits with your in-laws to boost your confidence.

---

[16] Flipping off your father-in-law on your way to the bathroom would be considered "causing a big scene."

#7 *They manipulate me with hidden messages and nonverbal communication.*

Take a look back at the boundary statements you made on this issue in the previous chapter. Here are some things you can SAY when your in-laws try to manipulate you with hidden messages or nonverbal communication:

_____ "Are you implying that you think I'm [rude / selfish / ungrateful]?"

_____ "I get the impression from what you just said that you think that I am inferior to you because I don't agree with you. Is that what you think?"

_____ "I can see by the look on your face that you don't approve of something I have said or done. Is there a problem?"

_____ "It seems from the tone of your voice that I have displeased you. What have I done to upset you?"

_____ "I can tell by your sigh that you are disappointed by my behavior. Let's talk about it."

_____ "I'd prefer if you just tell me what you need from me instead of rolling your eyes."

Here are some things you can DO when your in-laws try to manipulate you with hidden messages and nonverbal communication:

_____ Pay attention to your feelings. It can be very difficult to recognize when you are being manipulated in a subtle way. When you feel angry, hurt, guilty, etc, figure out why you feel that way. Don't ignore those feelings! When your inner voice warns you that you are about to be manipulated, ask yourself the following questions. *What did my in-laws just say/do? What did they really mean? Did they say/do that in order to get me to do something for them?*

_____ Excuse yourself from the room if you start to get the feeling you are being manipulated and you need a few moments to figure out what is really happening.

_____ Maintain your confidence. Remind yourself that just because they imply you are [rude / selfish / ungrateful] doesn't mean you are. If you second-guess yourself, then you will be easier to manipulate.

_____ Be careful you don't fall into your old pattern of reacting to their manipulative tactics. Don't make excuses, don't defend yourself, don't apologize, and don't criticize your in-laws.

_____ Call attention to your in-laws' nonverbal communication. If your father-in-law thinks he is being sneaky by manipulating you with the frown on his face, then respectfully ask him why he is frowning. He won't expect you to have the courage to talk to him about his frown, and he'll realize you aren't going to be so easily manipulated anymore.

_____ Don't let them have the last word. If your mother-in-law implies something negative about you, respectfully ask her what she means by that comment. This will catch her off guard and make her realize you know what she is doing and you won't tolerate it. If you can get her to admit out loud what she really thinks, then you can address the issue and any false belief surrounding it.

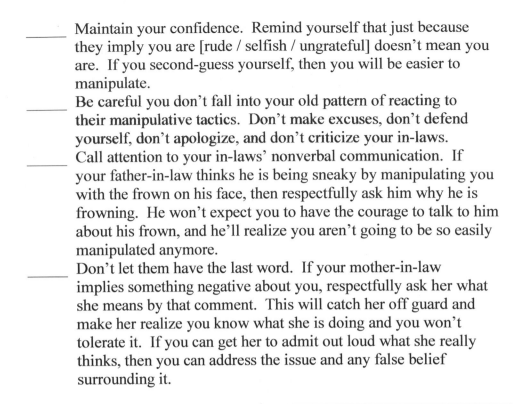

By respectfully calling attention to your in-laws' hidden messages and nonverbal communication, you are taking steps toward gaining your husband's loyalty. For years your husband has been stuck in the pattern of believing everything his parents imply without stopping to think about whether or not they are right. His parents have been able to manipulate him into thinking and/or doing things just by looking at him a certain way or using a certain tone of voice. Your husband probably has no idea this is happening. When you bring everything out in the open, your husband can see what is really going on…that his parents' ways of communicating are immature and unhealthy. By confronting his parents when they imply negative things about you, you are doing what's in your power to help your husband form his own opinion of you without being influenced by their negative opinion of you. Take advantage of opportunities to disrupt his family's unhealthy patterns of relating. By doing so, you will pave the way for new, healthy communication patterns which will play a big part in gaining your husband's loyalty.

#8 *They expect me to call them "Mom" and "Dad."*

Take a look back at the boundary statements you made on this issue in the previous chapter. In those statements, you addressed the following issues: (1) whether or not you are willing to call your in-laws "Mom" and "Dad" and (2) what you would like to start calling them from now on.

Here are some things you can SAY when your in-laws want you to call them "Mom" and "Dad" (or "Mr." and "Mrs."):

_____ "I'm flattered that you want me to call you 'Mom' and 'Dad,' but I'd feel more comfortable if we all called each other by our first names."[17]

_____ "I know I usually call you 'Mom' and 'Dad' (or 'Mr.' and 'Mrs.'), but I'd feel more comfortable if we all called each other by our first names from now on."

_____ "I'd like to call you by your first names since we're family now."

---

[17] If you are *not* comfortable calling your in-laws by their first names, then my advice is to get over it. The sooner you start calling them by name, the sooner you'll start feeling comfortable doing so. Don't act sheepish when you address them by their first names; speak clearly and with confidence.

#9 *My mother-in-law expects me to be the daughter she never had.*

Take a look back at the boundary statements you made on this issue in the previous chapter. In those statements, you addressed the following issues: (1) how often you are willing to talk on the phone with her, and (2) **how often you are willing to go on outings with her.**

Here are some things you can SAY when your mother-in-law invites you to do something you'd rather not do:

_____ "Thanks for the invitation, but I'm going to have to pass."
_____ "I can't meet you for lunch this Sunday. In fact, I'm not going to be able to keep meeting with you every weekend anymore. Is there a day next month you'd like to get together instead?"
_____ "I'm flattered that you treat me as if I were your own daughter, but unfortunately we have different expectations for our relationship. I'm sorry to disappoint you, but I need more space."

Here are some things you can DO when your mother-in-law invites you to do something you'd rather not do[18]:

_____ Decline the invitation tactfully[19].
_____ Plan other things in advance.
_____ Be honest about how the two of you have different expectations about your relationship.

---

[18] If none of these ideas work for you, then find someone who looks like you and pay her to hang out with your mother-in-law.
[19] "I'd rather eat my own vomit," is not a tactful way to decline an invitation.

#10 *My mother-in-law gossips about me to my husband, friends, and other family members.*

Take a look back at the boundary statements you made on this issue in the previous chapter. Here are some things you can SAY to the people who are listening to your mother-in-law gossip about you[20]:

_____ "It must put you in an awkward position when my mother-in-law gossips to you about me. The next time that happens, would you please encourage her to talk to me directly instead of putting you in the middle?"

_____ "I need to apologize to you because in the past I have listened to my mother-in-law gossip about you. I want you to know I won't do that again. Since she gossips to me about you, I suspect she also gossips to you about me. I'd appreciate it if from now on you'll refuse to participate in that."

Here are some things you can SAY to your mother-in-law when you discover she has gossiped about you to other family members, friends, and/or husband:

_____ "I know that sometimes you say negative things about me to others, and I'll admit that sometimes I say negative things about you too. I don't like it when you gossip about me and I'm sure you don't like it when I gossip about you. I hope we can behave like more mature adults from now on and come to each other directly when we are upset about something instead of talking behind each other's backs."

_____ "I want you to know that I know you said something negative about me to [a friend / a member of the family / my husband]. I would prefer that from now on when you have a problem with me, you'll discuss it with me directly instead of talking to others about it."

_____ "I want you to know I'm aware that you said something negative about me to [a friend / family]. I have asked that person not to listen to you gossip about me in the future."

---

[20] I will suggest more specific ways to confront your husband about this in the chapter entitled "Are We There Yet?"

_____ "I know that sometimes we disappoint each other. Sometimes I say negative things about you to my husband, and sometimes you say negative things to him about me. But I've come to realize that puts him in the awkward position. I hope in the future you and I will talk to each other directly instead of putting him in the middle."

If there things on your list that I have not addressed, take time now to write down what to say and do to enforce your boundaries on that issue. If possible, read more books on the subject to give you ideas and/or seek the help of a counselor, wise friend, or relative who has gone through the same challenges.

Refer to your list of boundaries and circle the three you feel need to be addressed first. Set a goal for yourself and write down a deadline for when you plan to say/do things to communicate and enforce those boundaries with your in-laws. After you've followed through on that, repeat the process until you have addressed all of your boundaries.

Chapter 5

We Don't Need No Stinking Boundaries
Preparing for a negative reaction from your in-laws and husband

Courage, sacrifice, determination, commitment, toughness, heart, talent, guts. That's what little girls are made of; the hell with sugar and spice.
--Unknown

A couple of years ago I opened a fortune cookie and the note inside read, "Hope for the best but prepare for the worst." There's nothing wrong with hoping your in-laws will respond in a positive way when you enforce a boundary, but the truth is they probably aren't going to like your new behavior. And that's okay. This chapter will (1) help you anticipate how your in-laws will react and (2) teach you what to say and do if they react negatively.

It's important to anticipate a negative reaction from your in-laws so you aren't caught off guard. When you set boundaries, they may…

- Act offended, insulted, and/or furious
- Gang up on you and defend each other
- Yell, cuss, sulk, pout, whine, and/or cry
- Give you the silent treatment
- Overreact and blow everything out of proportion (for example, you screen a call from your mother-in-law and then later she asks why you hate her)
- Try to make you feel guilty for enforcing a boundary
- Tell you boundaries aren't necessary between family members
- Accuse you of being selfish and disrespectful (ironically, your in-laws are probably the ones being selfish and disrespectful)
- Try to convince you that *your* behavior is the problem, not theirs
- Try to make you feel guilty for rocking the boat (for example, they may say, "Let's all just be cheerful and stay positive")
- Refuse to honor your boundary and then tell you not to be upset about it (for example, they ask if they can come visit you on Easter weekend and you tell them that weekend won't work but they say they are coming anyway and that you need to have a good attitude about it)
- Quote scripture out of context in order to prove you are wrong and they are right (for example, they might say "children should respect their elders" or "forgive and forget")
- Feel threatened by your desire for change and therefore try harder to control you
- Try to negotiate with you about your boundary (for example, you tell them you won't be answering the phone after 9PM anymore and they try to pressure you into changing the time to 10PM)

- Test you to see how serious you are about your boundary (you may have seen your kids do this; don't be surprised if your in-laws do it too)

The next few pages of this chapter will suggest specific things for you to say if your in-laws react in a negative way.

#1 *They call too early, too late, and too often.*

Let's say you have already enforced your phone boundaries by screening your in-laws' calls and/or letting them know you prefer they call within certain times of the day. Here are some reactions you could expect from in-laws with healthy attitudes:

- "Sure, I'll be glad to keep my calls after 9AM on Saturdays so you can sleep in."
- "No problem, dear. I don't expect you to answer my calls if you're in the middle of dinner. I screen my calls during dinnertime too."
- "I love to talk to you, but I don't want you to feel smothered. I'll just call you once a week now instead of every day. Thanks for letting me know how you feel."

Here are some reactions you could expect from in-laws with unhealthy attitudes, along with some great ways for you to respond:

In-laws: "I called you this morning but you didn't answer the phone."
You: "You're right."[1]

In-laws: "How dare you tell us you won't answer our calls after 10PM!"
You: "I'm sorry you don't approve[2], Harry, but I won't answer your calls after 10PM."

In-laws: "It's awfully disrespectful for you not to answer our calls during the dinner hour."
You: "I'm sorry you feel that way[3], but I still won't be answering the phone then."

---

[1] If they fish for information, don't give it to them. They don't need to know the reasons behind your actions. The less information you give them, the less they will be able to control you.
[2] Notice that I'm not suggesting you say you're sorry for having a boundary, but rather that you are sorry they don't approve of your boundary.
[3] Again, notice I'm not suggesting you apologize for being disrespectful, but rather that you are sorry they think you are being disrespectful.

In-laws: "I guess you just don't have time for us anymore (sniff sniff)."
You:　　"I'm sorry you're upset, Helen, but I still need for you to keep
　　　　your calls before 9PM."

Notice the importance of (1) acknowledging when your in-laws are angry, disappointed, disgusted, and/or sad but then (2) restating your boundary to show you aren't going to ignore your needs in order to gain their approval or keep them happy.

#2 *They invite themselves over and drop by unannounced.*

Let's say you have already enforced boundaries with your in-laws by saying/doing things to discourage them from inviting themselves over and dropping by unannounced. Here are some reactions you could expect from in-laws with healthy attitudes:

- "From now on, I'll call first instead of dropping in unexpectedly. I didn't realize you preferred that. Thanks for letting me know."
- "I didn't realize this was an inconvenient day/time for you. That's no problem. Just call me when you want to get together."
- "We're looking forward to visiting you in May. We'll be glad to stay in a hotel. Could you recommend one to us?"

Here are some reactions you could expect from in-laws with unhealthy attitudes, along with some great ways for you to respond:

In-laws: "I don't see why we can't drop by when we want. After all, we're family."

You: "I realize we're family, Harry, but I still need for you to call before coming over."

In-laws: "Next weekend may not be convenient for you, but we're coming anyway because that's when it is convenient for us."

You: "Next weekend just isn't an option, Helen, and I'm not willing to discuss that anymore. You are welcome to come the following weekend."

In-laws: "Why should we have to stay in a hotel? Is that any way to treat family?"

You: "I'm sorry you're upset, Harry, but I still need for you to stay in a hotel."

In-laws: "But I'll be lonely if I don't come see you every day."

You: "I don't want you to be lonely, Helen, but I still need you not to come over every day. Have you considered taking that painting class at the community college? I bet you'd meet some nice, new friends."

#3 *They beg __us__ to come visit __them__ all the time . . . especially during the holidays.*

Let's say you have already enforced your boundaries by communicating your needs about the frequency and length of your visits. Here are some reactions you could expect from in-laws with healthy attitudes:

- "I'll miss you on Saturday, but I understand you already have other plans."
- "We'll miss you on Thanksgiving, but we hope you have fun with your family!"
- "We'll miss our regular Sunday brunches with you, but it might be fun to get out of a rut and try doing new things. Thanks for inviting us to the movies Friday night; we're looking forward to it."
- "If you can only stay for three days, that's fine. Do whatever works with your schedule. We're just happy you're coming!"

Here are some reactions you could expect from in-laws with unhealthy attitudes, along with some great ways for you to respond:

In-laws: "You simply must spend Christmas at our house! You know it's tradition for all of our kids to come here for the holidays."

You: "I'm sorry you're upset, Helen, but we have our own family now and we are going to start our own traditions."

In-laws: "We can't possibly wait until June to see you. Why can't you come see us sooner?"

You: "I'm sorry you're disappointed, but we're sticking with our plan to come in June."

In-laws: "What do you mean you are only staying for three days? We haven't seen you for almost a year, and now you're only staying for three days"?

You: "I'm sorry you don't approve, Harry, but we won't stay longer than three days."

A WIFE'S GUIDE TO IN-LAWS

In-laws: "I don't see why you can't keep coming over for brunch on Sundays."

You: "I'm sorry you don't understand, Helen, but we won't be coming over every Sunday anymore."

In-laws: "I know you already said you won't come to visit, but I really think you should reconsider."

You: "Helen, 'no' doesn't mean 'ask me again until I say yes.' I'm not willing to discuss it anymore. Is there something else you'd like to talk about instead?"

#4 *They give unwanted advice and meddle in things that aren't their business.*

Let's say you have already enforced your boundaries by discouraging your in-laws from giving unwanted advice and meddling in your business. Here are some reactions you could expect from in-laws with healthy attitudes:

- "I'm sorry my advice gave you the impression I think you aren't capable of making a good decision on your own. That's not how I feel at all. You have made great decisions in the past and I have no doubt you'll continue to do so."
- "I had no idea it bothered you when I gave you advice about that. I know I can get too bossy sometimes. I'll try to keep my opinions about that to myself next time."
- "I'm sorry I meddled in your finances. I know that's none of my business. I'll try to stay out of it from now on."

Here are some reactions you could expect from in-laws with unhealthy attitudes, along with some great ways for you to respond:

In-laws: "We're older than you, so we know what's best for you."
You: "I understand how you might see it that way, Harry, but the decision is still up to me."

In-laws: "We're just trying to look out for you."
You: "I know you have good intentions, but it's not your responsibility to look out for us anymore now that we are adults, Helen. This is our decision."

In-laws: "Why won't you tell me how much you paid for your new television? I'm family; I have a right to know."
You: "I'm not willing to discuss our finances with you, Helen."

In-laws: "Why wouldn't you want my advice on how to raise your child? I raised my own kids and they turned out great."
You: "You're right, you did a great job raising your kids, Helen. But these are my kids and I'm going to raise them the way I think is best."

#5 *They control us with money.*

Let's say you have already enforced your boundaries by saying/doing some things to achieve financial independence. Here are some reactions you could expect from in-laws with **healthy attitudes**:

- "We've enjoyed having you live with us, but we understand your desire for a place of your own."
- "I sure have loved providing daycare for you, but if you want to try something different for awhile then I support that. They are your kids and you make good decisions when it comes to them."
- "It sounds like you're trying to make some wise financial decisions. We support you in whatever you decide to do about the house, car, etc."
- "You have been a great employee and I hate to see you go, but I understand your desire to try something new and I wish you the best of luck."

Here are some reactions you could expect from in-laws with **unhealthy attitudes**, along with some great ways for you to respond:

In-laws: "You want to start paying someone else to watch MY grandkids? No, I won't let some stranger watch my babies."

You: "I'm sorry you don't approve, Helen, but this isn't your decision. We're going to have someone else watch our kids from now on[4]."

In-laws: "What do you mean you don't want our financial help anymore? You are so ungrateful!"

You: "I'm sorry you feel that way, Harry, but I won't be accepting financial help from you anymore."

In-laws: "You can't quit working for me! This is a family-owned business and I don't want to hire some stranger to take your place. I've invested a lot of time and money in you. I really need you to stay."

You: "I'm sorry you're disappointed, Harry, but this is my decision.

---

[4] Notice I use the pronoun "we." If you and your husband aren't in agreement about this, then don't speak as if you are.

#6 *They make hurtful comments and then say they're only teasing.*

Let's say you have already enforced your boundaries by saying/doing things to limit teasing by your in-laws. Here are some reactions you could expect from in-laws with healthy attitudes:

- "I'm sorry I hurt your feelings."
- "I guess my comment was pretty insensitive. Please forgive me."

Here are some reactions you could expect from in-laws with unhealthy attitudes, along with some great ways for you to respond:

In-laws: "You are way too sensitive. Stop overreacting all the time."
You: "You're entitled to your opinion, Harry, but I still need for you to stop teasing me about that."

In-laws: "I was just teasing you. Lighten up!"
You: "I can see we don't agree on this, Harry, but if you tease me about this again I will leave the room."

#7 *They manipulate me with hidden messages and nonverbal*
   communication.

   Let's say you have already enforced your boundaries by
confronting your in-laws when they try to manipulate you with hidden
messages and nonverbal communication.
   Here is a reaction you could expect from in-laws with healthy
attitudes:

- "You're right, I do tend to [sigh / roll my eyes / shake my head]
  instead of just saying what's on my mind. I'll try to be more direct
  with you in the future."

Here is a reaction you could expect from in-laws with unhealthy
attitudes, along with a great way for you to respond:

In-laws: "Of course I'm giving you the silent treatment! You haven't
          come to visit me for six months and you wonder why I'm not
          talking to you"?
You: "I'm sorry you're disappointed, Helen, but in the future I need
          for you to say what is bothering you instead of giving me the
          silent treatment."

#8 *They expect me to call them "Mom" and "Dad."*

Let's say you have already enforced your boundaries by calling your in-laws something other than 'Mom' and 'Dad'. Here are some reactions you could expect from in-laws with healthy attitudes:

- "Hearing you call us by our first names will take a little bit of getting used to, but we're willing to give it a try."
- "We love having you call us 'Mom' and 'Dad,' but there's no reason you can't call us by our first names if that's what you prefer."

Here are some reactions you could expect from in-laws with unhealthy attitudes, along with some great ways for you to respond:

In-laws: "It would really make us sad if you called us anything else besides 'Mom' and 'Dad.' After all, we're family now."
You: "I'm sorry you're disappointed, but I'm not willing to call you 'Mom' and 'Dad' anymore."

In-laws: "What do you mean you aren't going to call us 'Mom' and 'Dad'?! Our other daughter-in-law has no problem with it."
You: "I'm sorry you don't approve, but from now on I'm going to call you 'Harry' and 'Helen.'"

In-laws: "It's very disrespectful of you to call us by our first names. You should respect your elders."
You: "You're entitled to your opinion, but we're all adults here. From now on I'm going to address you by your first name since you call me by my first name."

#9 *My mother-in-law expects me to be the daughter she never had.*

Let's say you have already enforced your boundaries about your relationship with your mother-in-law. Here are some reactions you could expect from in-laws with healthy attitudes:

- "If you'd like to just get together once a month instead of twice a week, that's fine with me."
- "I guess we just have different expectations about our relationship. Thanks for being honest with me."
- "I'm disappointed you don't want to have as close a relationship with me that I want with you. But I'll try to find other ways to get my needs met."

Here are some reactions you could expect from in-laws with unhealthy attitudes, along with some great ways for you to respond:

Mother-in-law: "What do you mean you won't come shopping with me? You should spend more time with me."

You: "I'm sorry you're disappointed I don't spend as much time with you as you think I should, Helen."

Mother-in-law: "I don't see why we can't get together once a week for lunch. That's what my friend Judy does with her daughter-in-law."

You: "I need for you to change your expectations of our relationship, Helen. I'll check my schedule for next month and we can get together for lunch then."

#10 *My mother-in-law gossips about me to my husband, friends, and other family members.*

Let's say you have already enforced your boundaries by saying/doing things to discourage your in-laws from gossiping. Here are some reactions you could expect from in-laws with healthy attitudes:

- "I'm sorry I gossiped about you. I hope you'll forgive me. From now on I'll talk to you directly."
- "Thanks for being honest. We'll have a better relationship if we both stop gossiping about each other and talk to each other instead."

Here are some reactions you could expect from in-laws with unhealthy attitudes, along with some great ways for you to respond:

In-laws: "Who told you I gossiped about you? I bet it was Suzanne. She's a liar."

You: "It doesn't matter who told me or what they said, Helen. What matters is from now on I need for you to come to me directly so we can work things out."

In-laws: "I didn't gossip about you."

You: "I'd like to believe that. I hope in the future you'll come to me directly when I've said or done something to upset you."

Unfortunately, there is only so much you can do to enforce this boundary. Once you consistently apply the suggestions I have given you, then all you can do is hope (1) your in-laws stop gossiping about you and/or (2) the people they are gossiping to refuse to listen.

If your in-laws respond in a negative way when you set boundaries with them, then it's important you don't stoop to their level. You'll gain respect for yourself if you can behave in a mature, dignified manner regardless of how others treat you. Also, if you are respectful toward your husband's parents,[5] then he'll be more motivated to transfer his loyalty to you.

> Imagine if roles were reversed and your husband was confronting YOUR parents about something. Would you want him to storm into their house with nostrils flared in anger? Or would you prefer he talk to them in a calm, respectful, dignified manner? Speak to his parents the way you'd want him to speak to yours.

Here are some general tips on how you can respond if your in-laws have a negative reaction when you set boundaries:

- Don't back down; stand firm on your (reasonable) boundaries.
- Don't apologize or give excuses for setting boundaries.
- Don't let them draw you off the subject; stay focused by stating your needs repeatedly.
- Don't argue with them or try to win their approval.
- Don't yell, cuss, flip them off, stick out your tongue, or flick boogers at them.
- Don't slip into an arrogant, judgmental, blaming, or condescending mode.
- Don't bombard them with a long list of hurtful things they have said and done in the past. (It is a good idea, however, to have a past situation in mind in case they ask you for an example of the behavior you are confronting them about.)
- Don't let their false thinking and unhealthy behavior go unchallenged. Don't let their false beliefs[6] and warped perspective of normal be the last thing your husband hears.
- Do speak in a clear, firm, calm voice.
- Do use their first names when speaking to them.
- Do maintain eye contact.
- Do fake confidence if necessary. Imagine you are a parent talking to a child, if that helps.
- Do maintain your integrity by speaking in a respectful, mature, tactful manner.

---

[5] Remember, these people you consider to be monsters are his parents and he loves them.

[6] I will discuss false beliefs in Chapter 7.

- Do try to remain calm; try not to get defensive.
- Do let them be upset; it's not your job to keep them happy.
- Do have the last word, even if you can't figure out what the last word should be until the next day; be persistent.

The main thing to remember about enforcing boundaries is that it is important to stop responding in the way your in-laws have come to expect you to respond.

Chapter 6

Are We There Yet?
Holding your ground after the confrontation

Whatever you do, you need courage. Whatever course you decide upon, there is always someone to tell you that you are wrong. There are always difficulties arising that tempt you to believe your critics are right. To map out a course of action and follow it to an end requires some of the same courage that a soldier needs. Peace has its victories, but it takes brave men and women to win them.
--Ralph Waldo Emerson

Have you ever noticed that amusement parks and vomit are closely linked? That's because in order to get the thrills we want, sometimes we have to feel yucky along the way. It's the same thing with confronting our in-laws. In order to experience the rewards that boundary setting brings, we have to go through some discomfort for a while. This chapter will (1) help you deal with what I call 'confrontation hangover' and (2) give suggestions on what to do if your husband freaks out when you set boundaries with his parents.

If you've just set a boundary with your in-laws and you feel shaky, faint, nauseous, and guilty, then there's a good chance you have a confrontation hangover. Don't worry; you won't die. This is completely normal. If you had the integrity to set boundaries in a respectful manner, then you achieved success even if your in-laws left the room sobbing or spewing profanity. <u>Success is defined by your actions, not anyone else's reactions.</u> Give yourself a pat on the back and buy yourself a treat.

CONFRONTATION HANGOVER DO'S AND DON'TS

- **Do** realize it's a good thing that you feel uneasy. It means you're growing up. It means you tried something new, and trying new things can be a little scary.

- **Do** realize that, if your in-laws (or husband) are mortified at your behavior, it doesn't mean you did something wrong. It just means you are redefining normal, and they'll get use to the new system eventually.
- **Do** stand firm on your boundaries instead of backing down.
- **Do** remember to be patient with yourself; the point isn't to get the confrontation perfect. The point is to start the habit of respectfully communicating your needs.
- **Do** learn from your mistakes. Brainstorm what you can say or do differently next time.
- **Do** realize that eventually setting boundaries will become easier for you to do, just like learning to drive a stick shift or riding a bike.
- **Do** be patient with your in-laws; they will probably need time to adjust to your new behavior. The way they are acting now may be very different than how they will act next month.
- **Don't** agonize and second-guess yourself over what you said during the confrontation.
- **Don't** believe you are a selfish, disrespectful person just because your in-laws get upset when you set a boundary.
- **Don't** consider your situation hopeless if you don't get instant results. The behavior patterns between you and your in-laws have been going on for years... these patterns will change gradually, not overnight.

Now you can be confident about future interactions with your in-laws. In the past you've probably dreaded contact with them because you were worried about being criticized, manipulated, trapped, etc. Perhaps you didn't know how to protect yourself before you started reading this book. I have good news for you. You don't need to be afraid of them anymore; they don't have any real power over you. You are capable of protecting yourself and your needs. All you have to do is anticipate their behavior patterns and plan new responses. You can stay one step ahead of them by setting boundaries instead of falling into your old patterns of behavior. Learn to endure the short-term discomfort of confrontations and be persistent in enforcing respectful, consistent boundaries, so you can accomplish your overall goal of gaining Hubby's loyalty.

For the last couple of chapters you've probably had a nagging question in the back of your mind: *"What should I do if my husband freaks out when I set boundaries with his parents?"* You have a legitimate concern, so let's talk about it. After reading previous chapters, you probably have a clearer idea of what your boundaries are and how to enforce them. But in reality, it's not that simple because it's not just you and your in-laws who are involved. Your husband can make it difficult for you to enforce your boundaries with his parents.

Here are four things you can do to make things a little easier on yourself and your husband.

1. **Set boundaries (with your in-laws) that you can enforce with or without your husband's support.** For instance, you *can* enforce the following boundary without your husband's support: *"I* am not going to be answering the phone after 9PM anymore." However, you *cannot* enforce this next boundary without your husband's support: *"We* are not going to be answering the phone after 9PM anymore." Like it or not, you can't control your husband's behavior. If your husband is home when your in-laws call, then he will likely answer the phone. It may drive you crazy, but as much as you want to, you can't make *him* enforce *your* boundary. All you can change is your behavior. You can control whether or not *you* talk to your in-laws on the phone; you cannot control whether or not *he* talks to them.

Likewise, you can't control whether or not he answers the door when they come over uninvited. You can only control whether or not *you* answer the door. You may also be limited on what boundaries you can enforce about becoming financially independent from your in-laws. For example, it's not practical to sell your house or car without your husband's cooperation. I'm not saying you should throw in the towel. Make it a priority to gain your husband's loyalty so that someday he will support you in enforcing boundaries with his parents[1]. Until then, keep enforcing your boundaries to the best of your ability.

2. **Tell your husband you enforced a boundary[2] before he hears it from his parents.** That doesn't necessarily mean you should tell him you are going to enforce the boundary *before* you actually do it. You can enforce the boundary and *then* tell him what you did as long as he hears it from you before your in-laws complain that you were rude to them. It's up to you whether to tell him before or after you set a boundary. Just be aware that if you tell him before you enforce the boundary, then you must be strong enough to follow through if he tries to talk you out of it.

3. **When you tell your husband you enforced a boundary with his parents, it's important to focus on your needs instead of criticizing him or his parents.** Stay calm and approach the situation with humor if you think he'll respond well to that. For instance you could hand him a bucket and then when he asks what it's for, say it's to catch his vomit after he hears what you did. Tell him you plan to start being more honest with his parents so you can have a better relationship with them. Assure him you communicated your boundaries to them in a tactful, respectful way. Tell him how you want him to respond when/if his parents complain because you set a boundary with them. Ask him to tell his parents to talk to you directly instead of listening to them gossip about you behind your back. Let him know you need his

---

[1] The next few chapters will give you specific suggestions on how to gain your husband's loyalty.

[2] He may not know what a boundary is so you can either try to explain it without going into a long psychological monologue or you can try to avoid using the word "boundary" altogether.

support even when he doesn't agree with you, and then tell him specifically what you want him to do in order to support you. Here are some examples of how to do that.

- "Honey, I need to be able to sleep, exercise, and eat without being interrupted by phone calls, so from now on I won't be answering the phone every time it rings. If your parents say they are offended by that, please encourage them to talk to me directly about it."
- "Sweetheart, I need to feel more in charge when visitors come to the house, so from now on I won't be answering the door if someone drops by unexpectedly. If your parents say they are offended by that, please tell them to talk to me directly."
- "Honey, sometimes I agree to visit your parents when I don't want to, and then I resent them for it later. I want to start having a more genuine relationship with them, so from now on I'm just going to visit them when I want to instead of when I feel obligated. I need for you to support me by not insisting I visit them this weekend."
- "In the past I've been mad at you because you wouldn't tell your dad to stop teasing me about being overweight. I was wrong; I should've just been honest and direct with him instead of expecting you to speak up for me. I want you to know I asked him to stop making comments about my weight. I need for you to support me by not saying I'm too sensitive."
- "Sweetheart, I've always called your parents 'Mom' and 'Dad' in the past but I'm going to call them Helen and Harry from now on. It's not because I'm trying to be disrespectful. I just feel more comfortable calling them by their first names. I need you to support my decision by not insisting I call them 'Mom' and 'Dad.'"
- "Honey, I've noticed sometimes you seem frustrated with me because I don't hang out with your mom as often as she would like. The truth is she and I just have different expectations for our relationship. I told her this morning I won't be able to have lunch with her on Fridays anymore, but that I'll go to a movie with her next month. I need for you to respect my decisions about how often I want to get together with your mom. I'd like for you to support me by not implying, to me or

her, that I'm a bad daughter-in-law just because I don't have the same expectations she does."

- "Sweetheart, I know you're put in an awkward position when I complain about your parents or they complain about me. I'm going to try to make things better for you, but I need your help. The next time I start to complain about your parents, please encourage me to talk to them directly instead. The next time your parents start to complain about me, please tell them to talk to me directly instead; tell them you aren't willing to be caught in the middle anymore.

4. **Accept the fact that your husband will probably get mad at you for setting boundaries with his parents.** Here's the thing… he's probably already mad at you because you don't get along with his parents, right? So why worry he'll be mad at you for taking steps to improve your relationship with them? If he's going to be mad at you anyway, then why not accomplish something while making him mad? Isn't it better to endure your husband's anger for a short time than to do nothing while your marriage dissolves? If he tries to talk you out of setting boundaries with his parents, follow through with it anyway. Is it more important to have your husband's constant approval or to do what needs to be done to improve your marriage? You can tell him you love him and value his opinion, but that you are going to do what you know is necessary to improve your relationship with him and his parents.

If you are consistent in setting boundaries with his parents, then don't be surprised if your husband eventually imitates your behavior. For example, your husband may believe that a good person always answers the phone, and a bad person screens calls instead. If so, then at first he'll think you are a bad person for screening phone calls. But if you stand firm and respectfully enforce your boundaries, then he may realize over time that it isn't necessary to always answer the phone in order to be a good person. He may envy the freedom you have to behave the way you want to instead of being controlled by the opinions and expectations of others. He may follow your lead in order to have relationships with others that are based on sincerity instead of obligation.

Chapter 7

Stop Making That Face
or It Will Get Stuck That Way
Exposing your husband's false beliefs

*The illiterate of the 21st century will not be
those who cannot read and write, but those
who cannot learn, unlearn, and relearn.*
                                    --Alvin Toffler

According to some guy on the Internet, the 2nd Law of Gun Safety is: *Never Point a Gun at Something You're Not Prepared to Destroy!* In the past you have probably directed your anger toward your husband and his parents whenever they behaved like jerks. But that hasn't done you any good, has it? That's because you're wasting your energy on yelling at Hubby and criticizing his folks when it would be better to focus on destroying the false beliefs causing the problems. This chapter will (1) teach you which false beliefs contribute to your husband's specific behaviors and (2) suggest things you can say/do so your husband will begin to question them. The next time your husband behaves in a way that makes you want to rip off your entire wedding finger, ask yourself what is causing him to behave that way. Once your husband is free from his prison of warped thinking, he will begin to transform from a guilt-ridden parent-pleaser into a confident, independent adult. It's impossible for me to list all of the false beliefs that contribute to your husband's behavior, but here are seven major ones:

1. My parents are superior to me even though I am an adult.
2. It's my parents' duty to judge me and give me advice.
3. My parents' needs are more important than my own.
4. It is important that I maintain just as close a relationship with my parents now as I did when I was young.
5. It's my responsibility to keep my parents happy.
6. I should continue to place my loyalty with my parents even though I'm married now.
7. It's better to pretend everything is fine, rather than rock the boat.

Now let's take a look at these false beliefs one at a time.

False belief #1: *My parents are superior to me even though I am an adult.*

If your husband believes that to be true, then his behavior will probably be like this:

- He rarely, if ever, considers the possibility that his parents might be flawed in their thinking or behavior.
- He assumes he is wrong whenever he thinks differently than his parents do.
- He tells you that you're wrong whenever you disagree with his folks.
- He believes you are rude, selfish, and/or disrespectful whenever his parents say you are rude, selfish, and/or disrespectful.
- If you and his parents describe a situation differently, he believes their version because to do otherwise would be calling his "perfect" parents liars. He accuses you of exaggerating, overreacting, and/or imagining things.
- He does everything they ask him to do because he thinks it would be disobedient to do otherwise.

True belief #1: *My parents are not superior to me; we are all equal adults.*

Once your husband believes this to be true, then his behavior will start to look this way instead:

- He will admit to himself that his parents aren't right about everything all the time, and that their behavior isn't always perfect.
- He won't assume you're wrong when you and his parents disagree about something.
- He will form his own opinions about you instead of believing his parents when they say you are rude, selfish, and/or disrespectful.
- He will consider your version of events when you describe a situation instead of assuming that his parents' perception is 100% accurate. He won't accuse you of exaggerating, overreacting, and/or imagining things.
- He won't feel the need to obey his parents.

Here are some things you can SAY to help your husband replace his false beliefs with the truth:

- "I know you've always looked up to your parents. I've always looked up to mine, too. But the truth is that sometimes parents are wrong, Honey. They have flaws just like everyone else."
- "Do you do everything your parents ask you to do because you think you have to obey them? You aren't a child anymore... you're an adult. You don't have to obey them any more than they have to obey you."
- "Honey, why do you feel it is disrespectful for me to disagree with your parents?"
- "Just because your parents don't think the same way you do doesn't mean you are wrong. There's no reason to be ashamed of your opinion, so stand by it. Your parents aren't right about everything just because they are your parents. You're an adult too, and your opinions are just as valid as theirs."

Here are some things you can DO to help your husband replace his false beliefs with the truth:

- Set an example by not bossing him around or belittling his opinions.
- Set an example by making sure you don't always assume your own parents' opinions are superior to yours and/or his.
- Encourage him to read the chapter entitled "Illegal Crack" because it will address his false beliefs in a way he can relate.

False belief #2: *It's my parents' duty to judge me and give me advice.*

If your husband believes that to be true, then his behavior will probably be like this:

- He turns to his parents for advice about everything and makes decisions based on whether or not they will approve. He values their input more than yours.
- He includes his parents in decisions that should be just between you and him (such as finances and child-rearing decisions).
- If he senses that his parents don't approve of how he is spending his time (for example, watching TV) he will either do something else instead or he'll keep doing it but feel guilty.
- If he senses that his parents don't approve of how he is spending his money, he will either stop buying what he wants or he'll keep buying stuff but feel guilty.
- If he senses that his parents don't approve of what he is eating, drinking, or wearing, then he will either feel guilty, change his behavior to please them, or hide things from them.

True belief #2: *It's my parents' duty to respect my right to make my own decisions.*

Once your husband believes this to be true, then his behavior will start to look this way instead:

- He will make decisions on his own without worrying whether or not his parents will approve. He will value your input more than theirs.
- Although he will seek his parents' advice occasionally, he will regularly make decisions without needing their approval.
- He will spend his time and money the way he wants to without worrying whether or not his parents will approve.
- He will eat, drink, and wear what he wants to even if his parents don't approve.

101

Here are some things you can SAY to help your husband replace his false beliefs with the truth:

- "I know you value your parents' advice, but sometimes I get the feeling you care more what they think than what I think. From now on, I need for us to make decisions as a couple."
- "There's no reason to hide that [junk food, beer, tattoo, earring, etc] from your parents. It's okay if they don't approve of everything you [drink, eat, wear, etc]. You aren't ten years old; it's not your parent's job to judge and correct you anymore."
- "Honey, why are you assuming that your parents know more about this than you do? You're a smart guy and you've done your research. If you think it's a good decision to [work for that company, buy that car, etc.], then don't let them talk you out of it."
- "I know you're feeling guilty right now, Honey, but it's not because you did anything wrong. It's because your parents are disappointed in your decision. I know you want their approval but part of being an independent adult means learning that it's okay if your parents are disappointed by your decisions."

Here are some things you can DO to help your husband replace his false beliefs with the truth:

- Turn to your husband for advice before you turn to your own parents.
- Anticipate when he'll want to ask his folks for advice about something, then familiarize yourself with the topic and discuss it with him before he has a chance to approach them for advice. The more prepared and informed you are about things, the more likely your husband will value your input and turn to you when making decisions.

False belief #3: *My parents' needs are more important than my own.*

If your husband believes that, then he will probably behave like this:

- He puts his own needs aside whenever they conflict with his parents' needs.
- He won't communicate his needs to his parents because he thinks that would be selfish and disrespectful.
- He ignores your needs whenever they conflict with his parents' needs.
- He accuses you of being selfish and disrespectful whenever your needs conflict with his parents' needs.
- He commits you to doing things with or for his parents without asking you first.

True belief #3: *My parents' needs are not more important than my own.*

Once your husband believes this to be true, then his behavior will start to look this way instead:

- He will value his own needs and communicate those needs to his parents.
- He will make your needs a priority over his parents' needs.
- He won't accuse you of being selfish or disrespectful whenever your needs conflict with his parents' needs.
- He won't commit you to doing things with or for his parents without asking you first.

Here are some things you can SAY to help your husband replace his false beliefs with the truth:

- "If you don't want to help your dad with his car tomorrow, then tell him that, Honey. He has other options. He can take it into an auto repair shop. Or he can wait until you can help him next weekend. It's okay if you don't put his needs before yours all the time."

- "If you don't want to cancel your dinner plans in order to help your mom move her couch, then tell her you can help tomorrow instead. Your needs are important too. Just because you don't drop everything doesn't mean you're selfish."

- "Sweetheart, I'm worried about you. You seem more concerned with pleasing your parents than taking care of your own needs. Why are you so hesitant to be honest with them when they ask you to do something you don't want to do?"

- "Honey, I've noticed that you tend to make your parents' needs more of a priority than mine, and I'm trying to figure out why that is. Is it because you feel their needs are more important than mine?"

- "I know you were just trying to be a good son when you told your mom I'd go over and help her tomorrow, but committing me to do things without asking me first means you care more about being a good son than a good husband. From now on I need for you to talk to me before you commit me to do something."

Here are some things you can DO to help your husband replace his false beliefs with the truth:

- Encourage him to say "no" sometimes to his parents, boss, co-workers, your parents, friends, children, salespeople, and telemarketers instead of pressuring him to say "yes" when others ask him to do something that conflicts with his needs. (Allow him to say "no" to you too!)
- Ask him questions that force him to question his own false beliefs such as, "Honey, are you worried your best friend won't ever speak to you again just because you said you can't give him a ride to the airport on Saturday?"
- Let your husband know you think his needs are important by (1) telling him his needs are important, (2) not pressuring him to always put your needs ahead of his own, and (3) not pressuring him to always put your kids' needs above his own.
- Compliment him whenever he is assertive with anyone.
- Let your husband make his own commitments. Don't commit him to doing things for his parents, your parents, friends, children, or yourself.

Your husband's parents aren't the only ones who taught him this false belief. Unfortunately most of society teaches that it's important to be a "nice guy" even if it means ignoring your own wants/needs. Why is it so hard for us to communicate honestly with people? Instead we have superficial relationships in which we commit to things we don't want to do and then feel resentful about it later!

False belief #4: *It is important that I maintain just as close a relationship with my parents now as I did when I was young.*

If your husband believes this to be true, then his behavior will probably be like this:

- He feels obligated to answer all of his parents' phone calls whether he wants to talk to them or not. He thinks it would be disrespectful to screen their calls or tell them he'll call back later.
- He expects you to answer all of their calls even if you're busy.
- He feels guilty if he doesn't call his parents as often as they think he should.
- He feels obligated to visit his parents every time they say he should visit them.
- He lets his parents invite themselves to your house and/or drop in unexpectedly on a regular basis.
- He continues his family traditions of spending every Sunday and/or every holiday with them because that's what they expect.

True belief #4: *It is important that I establish independence from my parents.*

Once your husband believes this to be true, then his behavior will start to look this way instead:

- He will feel free to decide whether or not he wants to answer the phone when they call. He'll realize it's not disrespectful to screen calls at inconvenient times.
- He will call his parents when he wants to, not when he feels obligated.
- He will visit his parents when he wants to, not when they expect him to do so. He will make his visits irregular instead of on a strict, routine schedule.
- He will tell his folks if it's an inconvenient time when they invite themselves over.
- He will form new traditions based on the needs of his new family instead of feeling obligated to follow all of his parents' traditions.

Here are some things you can SAY to help your husband replace his false beliefs with the truth:

- "Honey, there's nothing wrong with choosing not to answer the phone when you're busy doing something else (or if you're not in the mood to talk right then)."
- "Sweetheart, are you planning to visit your parents this weekend because you *want* to or because you feel obligated to? I thought you wanted to go golfing with your buddies on Saturday. There's no law saying that, in order to be a good son, you have to visit your parents every time they think you should."
- "Honey, there's nothing selfish or disrespectful about telling your folks we don't have time to hang out with them tonight because we have other plans. Hopefully next time they'll call first before dropping by so they don't waste a trip."
- "Honey, if you'd rather stay home and watch football then do that. I realize your parents' tradition is to spend Sundays at their house, but you don't have to follow their traditions for the rest of your life. You're an adult now and it's time to start your own traditions."
- "Your parents taught you the importance of family closeness, but don't forget the importance of independence and freedom of choice. If you find that you're always hanging out with your parents when you'd rather be elsewhere, then you don't have family closeness. What you have is a suffocating relationship based on obligation, resentment, and dishonesty."

Here are some things you can DO to help your husband replace his false beliefs with the truth:

- Encourage your husband to screen calls from his parents, your parents, friends, and telemarketers when he doesn't have the time or desire to talk to them.
- Encourage your husband to say "yes" when he *wants* to get together with his parents, your parents, or friends, but to say "no" when he'd only be going out of obligation.
- Get your husband and kids together to brainstorm some fun, new traditions.

False belief #5: *It's my responsibility to keep my parents happy.*

If your husband believes this to be true, then his behavior will probably be like this:

- He revolves his social life around his parents because they get upset if he doesn't.
- He spends his time (or money) trying to keep his parents happy but it seems that no matter what he does, it's never enough.
- He ignores his needs and does whatever his parents want because he can't stand to make them sad or lonely.
- He won't make a decision his parents don't approve of because he doesn't want to stress them out.
- He makes important decisions, such as where to work and where to live, based on what he thinks will make them happy.
- He assumes he has done something wrong whenever his parents are unhappy, disappointed, angry, or lonely.
- He expects you to go along with his parents' wishes, regardless of your needs, so you don't upset them.
- He gets furious with you whenever you do something that upsets his parents.

True belief #5: *It's not my responsibility to keep my parents happy.*

Once your husband believes this to be true, then his behavior will start to look this way instead:

- He'll realize his parents have the ability to find happiness on their own instead of depending on him. They can find their own friends, get a hobby, get a new pet, take a class at the community college, be a volunteer for the community, etc.
- He will realize he doesn't need to waste his time (or money) trying in vain to keep them happy.
- He will take care of his own needs even if it makes his parents sad or lonely[1].

---

[1] I'm not saying your husband should NEVER put his parents' needs above his own. I'm just saying it's not healthy for your husband to constantly bend over backwards to keep his parents' happy at the expense of his own needs (or yours).

- He will base his decisions on what he thinks is best instead of how it will make his parents feel.
- He will realize it's probably not his fault whenever his parents are unhappy, disappointed, angry, or lonely.
- He will understand it's probably not your fault whenever his parents are unhappy, disappointed, angry, or lonely.
- He will value your needs and won't get mad at you when you don't go along with his parents' wishes.

Here are some things you can SAY to help your husband replace his false beliefs with the truth:

- "Honey, I know you feel guilty for not spending more time with your mom. But you need to realize that if she's lonely, then that's because she is *choosing* to be lonely, not because you aren't spending enough time with her. Perhaps you could encourage her to [join that sewing club at the community center] to improve her social life."
- "It's important to take care of your own needs even though that may mean your parents will get sad or lonely."
- "Honey, I hope you'll do what you think is best for your [kids / career / marriage / health]. I know you're worried your parents might be upset about your decision, but you aren't responsible for their happiness. You'll still be a great son even if you decide to go through with this decision."
- "Honey, I get the impression you feel it's my fault your parents are [unhappy, disappointed, angry, lonely]. Is that how you feel?"
- "Honey, it seems you think I have a responsibility to keep your parents happy but that simply isn't true. I'm not going to ignore my needs just so they don't get upset."

Here are some things you can DO to help your husband replace his false beliefs with the truth:

- Gather some information about what college classes, clubs, and/or volunteer opportunities are available in your area by checking out the newspaper, local magazines, or the Internet. Share your findings with your hubby and maybe he'll want to suggest specific ideas to his parents about how they can improve their social lives.
- Help your husband realize he doesn't need to spend a lot of time (or money) trying to keep his folks happy. The next time his parents ask a favor of your husband, brainstorm with him and encourage him to suggest other ways for his folks to get their needs met without depending on him. For example, if his mom calls and asks him to mow the lawn, let him know he could suggest that she hire the neighbor boy to mow the lawn from now on.

False belief #6: *I should continue to place my loyalty with my parents even though I'm married now.*

If your husband believes this to be true, then his behavior will probably be like this:

- He makes decisions to please his parents because he thinks he is betraying them whenever he places his loyalty with you.
- He tries unsuccessfully to please his parents and you at the same time. He feels pulled in two directions, and he releases this frustration on you.
- He listens to his parents gossip about you. He becomes a messenger between them and you. He hates being caught in the middle but he doesn't know what to do about it.

True belief #6: *It's very important to transfer my loyalty from my parents to my wife.*

Once your husband believes this to be true, then his behavior will start to look this way instead:

- He will make your needs a priority even if his parents feel he is being disloyal for doing so.
- He will refuse to listen to his parents gossip about you; instead he will encourage them to talk to you directly

Here are some things you can SAY to help your husband replace his false beliefs with the truth:

- "Honey, I get the impression from your behavior that you think it's more important to honor your parents than to cherish your wife. Honoring your parents doesn't mean making their needs a priority over mine. You can make my needs a priority while still being a great son. As long as you love and treat them with respect, then you are honoring them even if you transfer your loyalty to me."

- "You seem frustrated because you must often decide whether to please your parents or me. You've always placed your loyalty with your parents in the past but, now that you're married, it's important to transfer that loyalty to your wife. If you make my needs a priority over theirs, then you will be less frustrated and our marriage will be stronger. Your parents may not approve, and you may feel guilty, but you won't be doing anything wrong by choosing to put your wife's needs first. That's what it means to be a marriage partner."

Here's what you can DO to help your husband replace his false beliefs with the truth:

- Set an example by making decisions to show your loyalty lies with your husband instead of parents or friends. Make his needs a priority even when it means disappointing others.

If your husband thinks his parents' behavior is wonderful, then use that to your advantage by pointing out how loyal his dad is to his mom. If your husband realizes that his dad is loyal to *his* wife, then maybe your husband will want to place his loyalty with you. Here's what I mean. Observe how your father-in-law reacts when someone teases your mother-in-law. Does he defend her by asking the person who teased her to leave her alone? If so, then tell your husband you think it's neat how his dad is loyal to his mom, and that it's important to be loyal to your spouse. Maybe the next time someone (like your father-in-law) teases you, your husband will ask him to leave you alone instead of accusing you of being too sensitive.

False belief #7: *It's better to pretend everything is fine, rather than rock the boat.*

If your husband believes this to be true, then his behavior will probably be like this:

- He won't confront his parents about their behavior because he'd rather pretend things are fine, rather than endure the discomfort of speaking the truth.
- He ignores his needs, instead of communicating honestly, in order to avoid tension with his parents.
- He doesn't want you to confront his parents about their behavior because he'd rather let things continue as they are, rather than risk awkwardness with his parents.
- He expects you to ignore your needs instead of speaking the truth because he's afraid of how his parents will react.

True belief #7: *It's better to improve my relationships with my wife and parents by working through the problems that exist.*

Once your husband believes this to be true, then his behavior will start to look this way instead:

- He will endure the short-term discomfort of confronting his parents' destructive behavior because he knows the end result will be a better relationship with them and you.
- He will be honest with his parents about his needs because he wants a more genuine relationship with them.
- He will encourage you to confront his parents about their behavior because he realizes it isn't wise to let things continue as they are.
- He won't get upset when you tell his parents your needs because he wants you to have a more genuine relationship with them.

Here are some things you can SAY to help your husband replace his false beliefs with the truth:

- "Honey, why are you hesitant to tell your parents the truth [about not wanting to visit them every Sunday]? Is it because you're afraid of what might happen if you do? What's the worst thing you think would happen if you were honest with your parents about your needs? What's the best thing that could happen?"
- "Aren't you tired of being dishonest with your parents? Aren't you tired of ignoring your needs? Would it be so bad if you just told your parents what you really thought about [doing all of their yard work]?"
- "If things stayed the same between your parents, you, and me for the next twenty years do you think that would be a good thing or a bad thing? Wouldn't you rather we get everything out in the open -- even if it were awkward for a short time -- so our relationships with each other could be better in the future?"

If your husband or his parents say it's better to "forgive and forget" than deal with relationship problems, then you might want to remind them there's also a verse about speaking the truth in love[2].

Here are some things you can DO to help your husband replace his false beliefs with the truth:

- Set a good example by confronting his parents (and your own parents) about their behavior when necessary.
- Set a good example by being honest with his parents (and your own parents) about your needs.

Are you encouraged now that you have a better idea of how to challenge your husband's false beliefs? I hope so. Be patient and don't expect your husband to wake up one week from now and say, "I had some unhealthy behavior patterns caused by false beliefs, but now I'm enlightened, so I'm no longer a slave to those beliefs. My behavior will be perfect from now on." You know as well as I do that your husband is no more likely to utter those words than he is to start making a quilt. He

---

[2] This is in Ephesians 4:15 in case you were wondering.

has held these false beliefs for many years and it may take quite awhile for him to realize they aren't true. Even when he finally does start to question his false beliefs, it won't be easy for him to suddenly implement new behavior patterns.

If you are persistent about applying this chapter but you don't see any results, then it may be that your husband needs to learn from someone else (in addition to you) that the beliefs and behavior patterns he learned growing up are unhealthy. Encourage him to read the chapter(s) in this book called "Naked Women" and "Illegal Crack". Or get a copy of the hilarious book called **Do Your Parents Drive You Crazy?** by Janet Dight. For a more serious book, suggest that he read **The Mom Factor : Dealing With the Mother You Had, Didn't Have, or Still Contend With** by Henry Cloud and John Townsend. Or perhaps he'd be willing to see a counselor who could help to challenge his false beliefs and offer a fresh, non-biased perspective.

When your goal is to destroy your husband's false beliefs, rather than take aim at him or his parents, then you will be that much closer to having the loyal husband you need.

Chapter 8

I am Rubber, You are Glue
Learning to control your anger

The real act of marriage takes place in the heart...
it's a choice you make not just on your wedding day,
but over and over again...and that choice is reflected
in the way you treat your husband or wife.
*   --Judith Viorst*

Y̲ou've probably seen this scenario on TV a hundred times. Two cowboys are pointing guns at each other. They are fighting about a woman. Or some land. Or who has the coolest belt buckle. Whatever it is, they are hopping mad at each other. They want to blow each other's brains out. Their faces are red and their foreheads are covered with beads of sweat…that's how mad they are. They have the option of saying, "You know what, this belt buckle isn't worth fighting over. How about I lay down my gun and you lay down yours and we'll go get some ice cream together?" But instead they decide to unload bullets on each other, and their corpses become the big story on the 10 o'clock news.

Now think about that scene again, only this time imagine it's you and your husband who are standing there. You aren't fighting over belt buckles. You're fighting about whether or not to go visit his parents this weekend. Both of you have a choice. You can start firing off nasty words at each other or you can maintain control of yourselves and work through the argument in a mature, respectful manner.

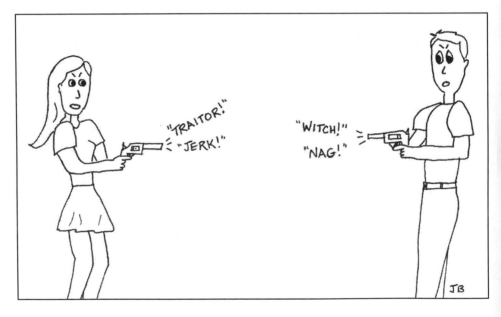

You're probably not proud of the way you've handled yourself during past fights with your husband about his parents. Perhaps he has learned to expect you to yell, cuss, slam doors, make accusations, etc. Your worst behavior probably brings out his worst behavior, and then arguments escalate out of control.

The good news is you don't have to live this way anymore. You can learn how to have a healthy argument with your husband. Why not be the first one to "lower your weapon" the next time you and your husband are having an in-law argument? If you can learn to change your behavior during the next argument about his parents, then he'll probably notice something is different. When your husband sees you handle yourself in a calm, mature way, then he will likely do the same. And then your best behavior can bring out his best behavior. Wouldn't it be great if, from now on, the two of you could talk as two civilized adults instead of escalating fights by shooting off hateful words toward each other? This chapter will teach you what to say during those dreaded arguments with your husband.

If you want to undo the unhealthy communication patterns you have now (for example, blaming, criticizing, yelling), then you need to learn new communication patterns. In other words, you need to stop behaving the way you have in the past, and behave in a new way instead. You need to start using statements that communicate your feelings, needs, and boundaries to your husband. By preparing statements ahead of time, you'll have something to say besides "I hate you" the next time you argue. It is possible to communicate your feelings, needs, and boundaries in a respectful manner even while you're angry.

Your husband may be more likely to transfer his loyalty to you once he realizes how his behavior makes you feel. He may be so concerned with taking care of his parents' feelings that he doesn't realize he is hurting your feelings in the process. You can prepare some "I feel" statements so the next time you have a discussion with your husband, you'll be ready to communicate how his behavior makes you feel.

An "I feel" statement should be non-threatening and non-judgmental. It should not be antagonizing. A bad example of an "I feel" statement is "I feel that your dad sucks." Your "I feel" statements should mention (1) a specific behavior of his[1] and (2) a specific feeling[2] you have as a result of his behavior. This is a good format to follow: "I feel [this emotion] when you [do this]." I will give you some good examples of "I feel" statements. But before I do that, I want to talk about "I need" statements.

Once you make an "I feel" statement to your husband, it's important to follow it up with an "I need" statement so he'll know what you'd like from him in the future. An "I need" statement shouldn't be about

---

[1] Note that I say *his* behavior, not his parents' behavior.

[2] List any feeling other than anger. He already knows you're angry.

revenge or manipulation. Its purpose isn't to criticize or antagonize. A bad example of an "I need" statement is "I need for you to tell your parents to go to hell."

Your "I need" statements should mention (1) a specific need of yours and (2) what he can start or stop doing in order to fill that need. Here are some good examples of "I feel" and "I need" statements.

Scenario #1:   *Your husband tells you he invited his parents over for dinner next Saturday.*

"I feel *unimportant* when you invite people to our house without discussing it with me first. I need for you to talk it over with me before you invite people to our home."

Scenario #2:   *Your husband insists that you skip your aerobics class on Wednesday evening because his parents want to get together then.*

"I feel *unimportant* when you care more about pleasing your parents than you do about pleasing me. I need for you to stop asking me to cancel my plans in order to please your parents."

Scenario #3:   *Your husband expects you to get up and go to church with his parents even though you have the flu.*

"I feel *unimportant* when you expect me to ignore my needs in order to please your parents. I need to know I'm the most important person in your life. You can fill that need by making my needs a priority over your parents' needs."

Scenario #4:   *Your husband accuses you of being selfish because you want to go to a movie with friends for your birthday instead of going to a party his mom wants to throw for you.*

"I feel *frustrated* when you tell me I'm selfish whenever my needs conflict with your parents' needs. I need to know you respect my needs. You can help by making my needs a priority even if that means upsetting your parents."

Scenario #5: *Your husband informs you his folks called to say they will be staying at your house for two weeks during the holidays.*

"I feel *unimportant* when you let your parents dictate when they will visit, how long they will stay, and where they will sleep. I need for you and me to make decisions as a team. You can help fill that need by asking for my input about when your parents can come visit us, how long they can stay, and where they will sleep."

Scenario #6: *Your husband committed the two of you to spending Easter in California with his folks.*

"I feel *unimportant* when you tell your parents we'll go visit them without asking me first. I need for us to make decisions as a couple. You can help fill that need by discussing it with me before you commit me to doing things with your parents."

Scenario #7: *Your husband expects you to have lunch with his parents every Sunday.*

"I feel *trapped* when you commit us to spending every Sunday with your parents. I need to be able to decide how and with whom I want to spend my free time. You can help fill that need by being willing to [spend this Sunday watching football at our house with friends] instead of being bound by your parents' traditions."

Scenario #8: *Your husband tells his parents you will be glad to paint their bathroom.*

"I feel *frustrated* when you commit me to do something for your parents without checking with me first. I need to be the one to decide whether or not I'm willing to do something for them. You can help fill this need by saying 'I'll check with my wife and get back to you' before you commit me to something."

Scenario #9:   *Your husband promised to go on a bike ride with you, but then changes his plans when his mom insists he spend the day fixing her computer instead.*

"I feel *disappointed* when you cancel plans with me in order to do something for your parents. I need for you to be a great husband instead of just a great son. You can help fill that need by telling your mom you'll fix her computer tomorrow since you already had plans with me today."

Scenario #10:   *Your husband accuses you of being rude to his mother because she said you took too long to write her a thank you card for your birthday present.*

"I feel *betrayed* when you accuse me of being [rude / selfish / disrespectful] just because your parents say I was [rude / selfish /disrespectful]. I need to know you see the best in me. You can help fill that need by giving me the benefit of the doubt instead of believing your parents when they say I'm [rude / selfish / disrespectful]."

Scenario #11:   *Your husband makes no effort to become financially independent from his folks.*

"I feel *trapped* when you insist on depending on your parents for everything. I need for us to become financially independent. You can help fill this need by [meeting with a financial advisor / sticking to a budget / moving out of your parents house]."

Scenario #12:   *Your husband insists on buying a Chevy (even though you want a Honda) because his parents think he should.*

"I feel *unimportant* when you value your parents' opinions over mine. I need to know you value my opinions. You can help fill this need by making decisions based on what you and I think instead of what your parents think."

Scenario #13: *Your husband is afraid to tell his parents the two of you won't be spending Christmas with them.*

"I feel *frustrated* when you aren't honest with your parents about our needs. I need to know you have the courage to be honest with your parents. You can help by telling them we have other plans for Christmas this year."

> Get a piece of paper and write down six in-law issues you and your husband tend to fight about often. Now come up with some "I feel" and "I need" statements by using the suggestions in this chapter, or coming up with your own. Save this list and I'll talk more about it at the end of the next chapter.

Even if you do a great job communicating your "I feel" and "I need" statements, that doesn't guarantee your husband will respond in a positive way. You should be prepared for a negative reaction from him so you'll know what to say/do if that happens. Your husband may say some things to draw the focus off your needs. It's important that you redirect the conversation back to your needs each time by saying things like this:

- "I can see how you'd feel that way, but I still need..."
- "You're entitled to your opinion, but I still need..."
- "We'll have to agree to disagree. I still need..."
- "You're right, but I still need..."

There are several different ways your husband might react when you tell him how you feel and what you need. He may give you the silent treatment, yell, cuss, interrupt, walk out of the room, drive away, defend his parents, or blame you. If your husband does these things, then you can respond by saying things like this:

- "I realize you're upset and don't want to talk about this now. I'll give you some time to think about all of this, and then we can talk about it this evening."
- "I understand you don't feel like working this out with me right now, but I need for us to discuss it when we've had a chance to cool down."

- "I want to hear what you have to say, but I'm speaking to you in a respectful tone and I need for you to do the same."
- "I want your feedback, but I need for you to wait and share it with me when I'm through talking."
- "I understand you left the room (or drove away) because you were too upset to talk about this right then. But we've both had a chance to cool down, so let's try it again in a more calm, respectful way. Let's agree that if either of us feels like we need to take a break to gain control of our emotions, we'll just say that instead of storming out of the room."
- "I realize it's instinctive for you to defend your parents, but when you defend them instead of trying to understand my viewpoint, we can't work through this problem together as partners."
- "I have contributed to these problems, but I'm not willing to take all of the blame."
- "Let's stay focused on the issue at hand."

Sometimes in addition to saying how you feel and what you need, it's necessary to draw a boundary with your husband. Let him know there are some behaviors that you aren't willing to overlook anymore because it is putting tension on your marriage. Here are some good examples of boundary statements:

_____ "I hope you'll back me up when I ask your parents to call before dropping by. I'm no longer willing to entertain them if you let them in when they drop by uninvited."

_____ "I hope, from now on, you'll talk to me first instead of letting your parents decide when they will visit and how long they will stay. If not, then I will go visit my sister during your parents' visits."

_____ "I hope from now on you'll ask whether or not I'm willing to visit your parents before committing us. Otherwise you'll have to go without me."

_____ "I hope you're willing to start new traditions with me instead of continuing to spend every Sunday at your parents' house. I'm not willing to do the same routine anymore."

_____ "I hope you won't join your parents in teasing me about my [nose / weight] anymore. But if it happens again, then I will leave [the house]."

_____ "I hope from now on you'll consider my perspective instead of assuming I'm the one to blame. I'm no longer willing to apologize to your parents for things that aren't my fault."

_____ "I hope in the future you'll consider my needs instead of telling me I'm selfish just because my needs conflict with your parents' needs. I'm no longer willing to ignore my needs just to keep you and your parents happy."

Unfortunately there are many times when it isn't possible or practical to enforce a boundary with your husband on a certain issue. In those instances, it's best just to keep communicating your feelings and needs in a calm, respectful manner. Now that you know what to say to your husband while you're angry, it's time to put that knowledge into action.

Chapter 9

Please Pass the Morphine
Surviving the pain of confrontation

*More marriages might survive if the partners realized
that sometimes the 'better' comes after the "worse."*
--Doug Larson

This chapter will advise you when, where, and how to have a discussion with your husband.

WHEN TO SCHEDULE A CONFRONTATION

You can choose when to confront your husband about a problem in advance, rather than wait for a fight to catch you off guard on a day you have PMS. Wouldn't you rather initiate a confrontation when you're feeling prepared, calm, courageous and well rested? There are a few things to consider when deciding on a good time to confront your husband. For example, don't approach him when either of you are hungry[1]. Or when he is in a hurry. Don't approach him when your two-year-old is screaming at the top of her lungs. Or when he's in the middle of watching his favorite TV show. Don't approach him in front of family or friends. Wait until he is alone, relaxed, in a decent mood, and the kids are in bed. If that's not possible, then use your best judgment (because if you wait for the perfect moment, you may be waiting forever).

You can include your husband in the decision about when to have a discussion. There are several ways you can go about doing that. You could just be straightforward and say, "Honey, I need to talk to you about something. Is this a good time?" (If he says no, then ask him when would be a good time.) I warn you, this approach may not be the best one because men hate to talk about relationship issues. In fact, most of

---

[1] We have a rule in our family to never discuss anything of importance on an empty stomach. It's a very, very good rule.

them hate to talk about anything other than sex, sports, and television. If you walk right up to your husband and say it's time to work out some issues about his parents, there's a good chance he will have a seizure.

I suggest you consider other approaches such as bribery, bartering, and/or humor. A small dose of bribery may be all you need to break the ice with your husband. You could say, "I bought this candy bar for you for two reasons. One, because I love you. Two, because I'm trying to bribe you into talking about some issues regarding your parents. When would be a good time to do that … now or after dinner?" He still won't be overjoyed about having a discussion about his parents, but chances are your grin and some chocolate will melt his defenses a bit. And don't underestimate the power of bartering. Who says you can't make this a win-win situation? You could say, "Honey, if you're willing to talk over some things with me after dinner, then I'll watch the kids Saturday so you can go golfing with the guys." If bribery and bartering don't appeal to you, how about using humor to lure your husband into a discussion? Write him a funny note and put it in the seat of his car before he goes to work.

Whatever you do, don't wait for him to initiate a confrontation with you. That would be like waiting for your dog to remind you it's time to go to the vet to get his shots. And don't expect your husband to be thrilled with the opportunity to strengthen your marriage. One day I approached my husband after a big fight about his parents and said, "We need to talk." His response was, "Crap." (That's when I learned that in the future I should barter with him when I wanted to discuss his parents.) If your husband responds this way, try not to take it personally. Don't read into it and think he doesn't love you, or that your marriage is unimportant to him. Realize he is a male and, therefore like most males, he would rather spend a day at the proctologist than talk about things such as feelings and needs. When you sense resistance from your husband, fight the urge to run away screaming. Just take a deep breath, tell him again that you need to talk about some things with him and ask him when he wants to talk[2].

Be ready for him to do whatever he can think of to avoid having a discussion with you. He may decide to apologize in order to get out of the discussion. Accept his apology with grace, but don't let him off of the hook so easily. Tell him you still need to discuss something with him

---

[2] Don't leave the question open ended. Give your husband two or three options such as "after dinner" or "right now" or "tomorrow evening."

and ask when he would be willing to do that. Be ready for him to give every excuse imaginable for why he can't commit to scheduling a time for this discussion. Don't let him postpone the discussion for more than two days unless he has a kidney stone. If he won't agree to a time, don't back down and don't let your emotions get the best of you. Just say, "Honey, talking about all of this isn't my idea of a great time either, but we owe it to ourselves to face our problems instead of pretending they don't exist. Our marriage is really important to me and I think it is to you, too. How about if we talk this over after dinner?" If he balks again, ask him "What will it take for you to sit down and talk things over with me? What can I do?"

If you try everything you can think of to get your husband to discuss problem issues with you but he refuses to talk or listen, ask him why he isn't willing to discuss anything with you. If he says it's because you are too angry all the time, then suggest a compromise. Tell him you'll go alone to see a counselor once a month about controlling your anger if he agrees to come with you twice a month to discuss the issues involving his parents.

WHERE TO HAVE THE CONFRONTATION

There are many places where the confrontation can take place…in your own home, at a park, at a restaurant, etc. Think about which setting would make the most sense for you. If you think your husband might walk out the door if you have the confrontation at home, then consider going someplace where it would be more difficult for him to leave. For example, you could have the discussion on a hiking trail. If you think you and your husband would be more likely to be more civilized to each other if you were at a restaurant, then go there. However, if you think there's a chance the two of you will cause an embarrassing scene, then consider talking things out on a walk through a neighborhood where you don't know anyone. If you think you and Hubby may need some anger management breaks during the confrontation, then consider taking your bikes to the park; you can talk awhile on a park bench, then ride bikes to blow off steam, then stop and talk again. Wherever you decide to talk things out with your husband, make sure it's just the two of you[3] and that you have some degree of privacy.

HOW TO HAVE A CONFRONTATION

Admit fault and apologize for what you have done wrong. Be humble and honest. Here are some examples of things you can tell your husband.

- "I'm sorry I overreacted when you told me your parents wanted us to spend Christmas at their house."
- "I'm sorry I have a bad attitude toward your parents. I'll try to work on that."
- "I'm sorry I let my anger get out of control earlier."
- "I'm sorry I gave you the silent treatment. I'll try to start doing a better job of telling you what I need instead of being mad because you can't figure it out on your own."
- "I'm sorry I said terrible things about your parents. I'm going to try to stop complaining to you about them."

Make it a habit to apologize to your husband whenever you are at fault. If he sees you are making an effort, then (1) he'll know you are trying to improve your behavior even though you may not get it right every time and (2) he'll be more likely to follow your example and make an effort to improve his own behavior.

Prepare your response for his apology. Your husband may decide to apologize to you because you've just apologized to him. You may be tempted to say something snotty or judgmental, but it's important to resist that urge. If you accept his apology in a kind manner, then he may be more likely to apologize to you again in the future. You may also be tempted to just accept his apology and drop the subject. But a brief exchange of apologies probably isn't going to be enough to effectively deal with the issue at hand. In fact, your husband may just be apologizing because he doesn't know how to deal with the problem on a deeper level. He may just be conditioned to apologize to whomever is upset at that time (either his parents or you) in an effort to win that

---

[3] That means no kids, parents, or friends should be present. The exception to this rule is if you want to meet with a counselor.

131

person's approval. Whether intentional or not, his apologies may have more to do with trying to keep you happy than feeling genuinely sorry for his past behavior. Unless the two of you discuss the issue on a deeper level, apologies by themselves probably won't bring you any closer to having a stronger marriage.

Start off with a positive statement. Use this opportunity to remind your husband that you love him and see the best in him. Here are some examples of what to say.

- "I love you."
- "You're my best friend."
- "Our marriage is important to me and I think it is to you too."
- "I know you have good intentions."
- "I think that most of the time you want to place your loyalty with me but that you just aren't always sure how to do that."
- "I'm confident that we can get through this."

Give him a reason to want to discuss the problem issue with you. Your husband is probably just as frustrated with things as you are. He wants you to get along with his parents. He wants to stop fighting with you. He wants to stop feeling trapped between you and his parents. Here are some things you can say to make him realize that discussing the problem issue is a win-win situation for everyone involved.

- "I think it's important to talk about [this issue] so that we don't continue to fight every time this comes up. Wouldn't you like it if we could stop fighting about this all the time?"
- "I know it's frustrating for you that your parents and I can't seem to get along. I think your parents and I will have a better relationship if you and I can come up with a compromise on [this issue]."
- "I'm sure you're tired of trying to keep your parents and me happy at the same time. Let's talk about [this issue] and come up with a solution so that you don't have to feel so frustrated all the time."

State your feelings and needs. This is the main purpose of having a confrontation. Refer back to the last chapter where I gave examples of sentences you can use to discuss specific feelings and needs. Your husband won't know how to express his loyalty unless you tell him specifically what you want him to say or do when a certain situation comes up in the future. If necessary, set some boundaries with him too (also discussed in the last chapter).

Let your husband vent his feelings. Your husband will probably be defensive when you tell him how you feel and what you need for him to do from now on. Don't worry; that just means he's human. In fact, it may be cause for alarm if he *isn't* defensive. For instance, if you tell him you need for him to take your needs into consideration instead of just focusing on what his parents want, and then he cheerfully says, "sounds great, wanna play tic-tac-toe?" then something isn't quite right. Either he wasn't listening or he's ignoring the problem in hopes that you'll go away. Encourage your husband to say what's on his mind. Find out what his needs and frustrations are. Validate his feelings. Listen to your husband without interrupting, arguing, blaming, getting defensive, or criticizing his parents. Your husband needs to vent his feelings of frustration and anger just like you do. He'll be more open to your perspective once he tells you his perspective. He'll be able to listen to you better when he isn't busy trying to think of what he wants to say in defense. It won't be fun to hear him get everything off his chest, but it's important for him to do that so you can move to the next level. You can take it! No one has ever died from being yelled at or criticized[4].

---

[4] Or if they have, I'm not aware of it.

Once he has spoken his mind and calmed down, then the two of you can move past the surface tension and get to the root of the problem issues at hand. When the two of you learn to talk to each other with the intention of working toward a solution, rather than verbally attacking each other, then you can make some progress.

> While it's important to let your husband get out his bottled up feelings, it's also important to let him know when he is treating you in an unacceptable manner. The last chapter suggests ways to respond to your husband when his venting becomes inappropriate.

Work toward a solution. Try to come up with a win-win solution if that's possible. The chapters called "Living as Friendly Vegetables" include worksheets to help you and your husband achieve compromises on common issues. Compromise is a big key to a successful marriage, especially when it comes to disagreements about in-laws. Choose to compromise if it will improve your relationship in the long run. For example, if your husband wants his parents to come visit your house for a week but you don't want them to come at all, suggest they come for three days and/or stay at a hotel. It's important to remember there's a difference between caving in to the pressure from your husband (and/or his parents) versus choosing to compromise because you want to communicate that you love your husband. Use your judgment about which boundaries to stand firm on, and which ones to be flexible about.

Take advantage of each potential fight and turn it into a way to improve your relationship with your husband instead of making it worse. For example, if your husband knows you aren't crazy about his parents, but you invite them for a surprise visit on his birthday, then he will realize you love him enough to do something you didn't want to do in order to make him happy. Instead of each of you refusing to be the first one to give in, initiate a truce by doing something that shows you love him more than you hate his parents. It will speak volumes to him and it will help to knock down the wall between the two of you.

Maintain your composure. The goal of a confrontation with your husband should be to gain his loyalty[5]. And since a high percentage of

---

[5] Confrontation is also about getting your needs met, but ultimately it's about gaining your husband's loyalty.

communication is nonverbal, it's important to remember that even though *what* you say is important, *how* you say it is just as important. In fact it's probably MORE important. Even if you can't remember one single prepared statement or response, just remember above all else, no matter what, to remain calm. And even if you do remember all of your rehearsed assertive statements, you'll only be effective if you speak in a non-threatening manner. Realize that if you seem full of rage and revenge whenever *you* talk to your husband, and in comparison his parents remain calm whenever *they* talk to him, your hubby will be less likely to want to transfer his loyalty to you.

Take breaks when necessary. There will be many moments when you will be tempted to tell your husband off, scream at him, poke him in the eyes, etc. But you must resist those urges if you are to succeed in gaining his loyalty. I'm *not* saying you should bottle up your rage and pretend it doesn't exist, because that's unhealthy. I *am* saying that, if at any point during the discussion with your husband you feel that your emotions are getting the best of you, take a short break to vent your feelings. You could excuse yourself to the restroom and use the time to gain your composure and re-focus on the issue at hand[6]. Or you could say, "Let's take a thirty minute break and then discuss this again. I need to get control of my emotions." Then do some physical exercise to release some of your pent up, negative energy. Yell at a photograph of your husband (outside of your husband's earshot). Or write an angry letter but don't give it to him. Don't let the short break turn into a long break, stretching into the next day or week. Return to the discussion as soon as you get control of yourself.

AFTER THE CONFRONTATION

After you've confronted your husband, you may think you failed because you didn't see any instant positive results. Your husband may say some hateful things to you during a confrontation. And you may assume that he meant what he said and that he'll always feel the same

---

[6] During the break, refer back to your list of "I feel" and "I need" statements if necessary. Refer back to your memorized responses to his anticipated reactions from the previous chapter.

way. Don't give up! Your husband may just need some time to digest
what you said. His initial reaction probably won't be his final reaction.
One time my husband and I had an argument that lasted for two days.
Names were called. Feelings were hurt. There was crying, blaming, and
yelling. And yet just when I thought I couldn't take anymore, my
husband said, "I'd give up my left nut to keep you happy." The next time
you are hyperventilating because your husband is driving you insane,
breathe into a bag[7] and remind yourself that things probably won't seem
so hopeless in a few hours.

Here are three questions to ask yourself to determine if the
confrontation was successful or not:

- Did you tell your husband how it makes you feel when he says or
  does a certain thing?
- Did you tell him specifically what you need for him to say or do
  from now on when certain problem situations come up?
- Did you speak as calmly and respectfully as possible?

The important thing is that you continue to establish a new pattern of
communicating with your husband in a respectful manner, even when
you'd rather shoot him with poisonous darts. You can't change the way
he speaks to you, but you can change the way you speak to him. It takes
two people to fight and if you choose to behave maturely, then he will be
influenced by your behavior eventually. Don't be afraid of having
arguments with your husband. Healthy arguments show that you aren't
ignoring your problems, and that's a good thing. The more disciplined
and courageous you are in initiating calm confrontations with your
husband, the fewer unhealthy fights you'll have. Remember that each
successful confrontation will bring you closer to achieving the goal of
gaining your husband's loyalty. If you can gain your husband's loyalty
by developing a habit of respectful conversations instead of emotional
screaming matches, then your in-laws will no longer be a threat to your
marriage.

---

[7] Paper, not plastic.

During the last chapter, you wrote down the six in-law issues you and your husband fight about most often. Find that paper now and decide when you want to talk to your husband about each issue. Prioritize the issues and make sure you take care of the most urgent issues first...the ones most harmful to your marriage.

Chapter 10

You Can Be My Wingman Anytime
Helping your husband develop new behavior toward his parents

Don't walk in front of me, I may not follow.
Don't walk behind me, I may not lead.
Walk beside me and be my friend.
                    --Albert Camus

L et's pretend that yesterday you confronted your husband about how you need to stop spending every Sunday with his parents. Let's give him the benefit of the doubt and assume he was very receptive to you and even suggested getting together with friends on Sunday. So here you are on cloud nine thinking your husband is no longer the putz he used to be. You're looking forward to enjoying the rest of your life with a loving, loyal husband. But wait. The phone rings and you hear your husband utter these terrifying words: "Yeah, Mom, we'll be there for brunch on Sunday. We're looking forward to it."

Of course you want to kick him in the kneecaps. But before you do that, it would be wise to stop and think about what just happened. You may be too seething mad at your hubby and his mom to realize you are part of the problem here. What did you do wrong? Well, let's start by looking at what you did right. If you applied what you learned in the last few chapters, then you did right by seizing opportunities to help your husband realize he has false beliefs causing unhealthy behavior. You did right again by respectfully showing your husband that some of his parents' behavior is unhealthy. And you did right by communicating your feelings and needs in a loving way. So then what you did wrong? Well you assumed your job was done. You figured that, once your husband learned he had false beliefs, he would then realize which of his behaviors were unhealthy and automatically know how to change them. You figured that, once he admitted his parents had unhealthy behavior, from then on he would know what to say and do to let them know he wasn't going to tolerate their unhealthy behavior anymore. Since your husband learned what your needs were and expressed a desire to meet those needs, you again assumed he would have the courage to tell his parents "no" whenever they wanted him to put their needs ahead of yours. Unfortunately it's not an overnight process, but there are some things you can do to help speed up the process.

Avoid criticizing your husband's parents. If your husband starts to realize his parents aren't perfect, don't assume he is now totally on your side. Don't start telling him everything you hate about his folks and think he'll agree they are horrible people. Your husband will probably be less likely, not more likely, to place his loyalty with you if you bad mouth his folks. After all, you wouldn't respond well if he criticized your parents, would you? Whenever it's necessary to talk about his parents' unhealthy behavior, do it in a non-accusatory way. Stay focused on working toward a solution that will bring you and your husband closer instead of trying to convince him his parents belong in an insane asylum.

Avoid criticizing your husband. You won't bring out the best in your husband if you tell him he acts like a gutless moron around his parents. Instead of verbally attacking him, speak gently about the way he behaves toward his parents. <u>Let him know that, although he isn't the only one contributing to the current problems, he is the key to the solution.</u> Help him understand it doesn't matter if his parents ever change their behavior; what matters is his *response* to their behavior.

Be empathetic. Before you start getting too upset with your husband for not standing up to his parents, think about how you felt the last time you said "no" to someone else in order to take care of your needs. Have you ever told your boss "no" when he really needed for you to pick up an extra shift? Or have you ever turned down a friend's request for a favor because it conflicted with your needs? Do you remember hearing disappointment in your parents' voices when you told them you couldn't come visit them? What were your emotions? Did you feel guilty for letting them down? Did you feel obligated to give them good excuses to justify why you didn't do what they asked of you? Did you wonder if you were a bad employee, friend, or daughter? Did you worry they wouldn't like you anymore? Did you fear you'd lose your job, your friend, or your parent's love? Were you tempted to just do what they wanted so you could avoid all of those bad feelings? Did you second guess yourself and wonder if you were wrong to make your own needs a priority? Did you wonder what co-workers, other friends, or other family members would think of you when they heard about your behavior?

If you can remember all of those feelings of guilt, fear, and insecurity, then you can appreciate how difficult it will be for your husband to stand up to his parents. It's important to be sensitive to what he's feeling instead of just demanding he march up to his parents and tell them off. The way you approach him, the tone of your voice, and the look on your face will either communicate that you are an unsympathetic, domineering nag or a compassionate, supportive partner. Tell him you know it isn't easy for him to stand up to his parents and ask how you can help.

Assure your husband that you don't expect him to be disrespectful to his parents. Your husband may be scared to confront his parents because

141

he thinks you want him to tell them to go to hell (which may secretly be true, but don't tell him that). He may think you expect him to walk up to his parents and say, "I hate you; you're bad parents.... you're controlling and manipulative... I love my wife more than you...I don't want to ever see you again." Let him know you realize he loves his parents. Let him know there are respectful, loving ways for him to let his parents know he won't tolerate their unhealthy behavior anymore. For instance, if your husbands' parents ask if you can come for the holidays, you may want him to say, "There's no way in hell we're going there for Christmas...my very wise and beautiful wife has enlightened me to the fact that you have emotionally abused us for years... when and if we ever decide to forgive you for all of the mental anguish you've caused us, we'll let you know...in the meantime, don't call or visit us... you'll be lucky if we ever come there for Christmas again."

But that's not realistic and your husband needs to know you don't expect him to be disrespectful to his parents. Your husband will be more likely to stand up for himself, and for you as a couple, if he can do that in a way he feels isn't disrespectful to his parents. In the past your husband has assumed he only had two options. Either he could place his loyalty with you and make his parents mad, or he could place his loyalty with his parents and make you mad. Let him know that he has a third option... he can be a loyal husband *and* a loving, respectful son. And that he has a chance to behave in a new way that will strengthen his marriage and enable him to have a more honest, adult relationship with his parents.

Assure your husband that you don't expect him to have a long, formal confrontation with his parents. If you tell your husband you'd like for him to start standing up for himself and for you as a couple, he may think you are asking him to sit down with his parents and have a two-hour discussion about an issue while his dad is yelling and his mom is crying. While it may be helpful to have a more formal confrontation such as that sometimes, often it's not necessary. Let your husband know he can improve the behavior patterns between him and his parents by learning some new things to say and do when opportunities arise. For example, he can simply get Caller ID and start screening his parents' calls instead of scheduling a formal meeting to tell them they call too often.

Think of ways to make it easier for your husband to speak up to his parents. Your husband will probably have an easier time saying "no" to his parents about something if he can say "yes" about something else. For example, your husband may dread the thought of having to tell his parents the two of you won't be spending Christmas with them. But it might be easier for him to tell them the bad news about Christmas if at the same time he can invite them to visit on Easter. Your husband might also have an easier time saying "no" to his parents if he can provide other options for them. Your husband may feel like he is leaving his parents in a bind if he says he can't come fix their computer tonight because he's going on a date with you. He'd probably feel better saying "no" to them if he could (1) give them a phone number to call to get their questions answered by a computer expert, or (2) tell them he can help them after work the following day. Another thing that might make it easier for your husband to say "no" to his parents is if he can show them in a different way that he cares for them. For instance, if he feels bad that he won't be flying out to spend his mom's birthday with her, suggest he send flowers on her special day so he can communicate that she is still important to him.

Give your husband specific ideas on what to say and do in order to develop more healthy behavior patterns toward his parents. Your husband may be willing to start responding differently toward his parents, but he isn't sure what to say or how to say it. Encourage him to read two chapters in this book that I wrote just for him: "Naked Women" and "Illegal Crack[1]." If you're thinking there is no way you'll ever get your husband to read those chapters, then start thinking more positively. There's got to be SOMETHING you can do to make him want to read those chapters…be creative[2]. Walk up to him with a grin and say, "I'd like to buy two hours of your time… I have something I want you to do that you won't want to do, so I'm willing to do something you want me to do in exchange…if you read two chapters[3] in this book this week, then I'm willing to watch the kids while you go hunting with the guys this weekend." If he says the only way he will read those chapters is if you run naked thru the neighborhood, then I suggest you start taking off your clothes. If you absolutely positively cannot get him to read those

---

[1] The chapter "Illegal Crack" has a section called *Good Things To Say to Your Parents.*
[2] For example, he might agree to let you read the chapters aloud to him if you aren't wearing clothes.
[3] Don't forget to mention that the chapters have cartoons and that one of the chapters is called "Naked Women."

chapters, then read them yourself and try to relay the information to him at the appropriate times. For more ideas on what your husband can say and do to interact with his folks in a healthy way, re-read the chapter called "Don't Stand So Close To Me" and adapt the statements so they become things your husband (instead of you) can say to his parents. You might also want to try going through the worksheets together in the "Living as Friendly Vegetables" chapters; they may help you brainstorm what to say and do to draw healthy boundaries with his parents.

Prepare your husband for his parents' reactions. Let him know he isn't responsible for his parents' feelings; they are. <u>If his new behavior is honest, loving, and respectful, and they *choose* to be hurt, angry, and/or offended, then that is their choice. It doesn't mean your husband did anything wrong.</u> It doesn't mean he is an unloving, disrespectful, selfish, or bad son. Help him think of ways to respond to his parents in an assertive way so he'll be prepared to handle them no matter how they react. See the chapter called "Illegal Crack" for ideas.

If you can learn to bring out the best behavior in your husband, then the problems with your in-laws will start to become a thing of the past. That doesn't necessarily mean his parents will stop having unhealthy behavior. It just means you and your husband will stop allowing their unhealthy behavior to have a negative affect on your marriage. For example, they can continue to expect you to spend every weekend with them, but if you and your husband unite and respectfully say "no", then they have no power over you. Isn't it nice to know you can have a successful, strong marriage even if your in-laws never change their behavior?

Chapter 11

How Many Forms of Birth Control Can I Safely Use at One Time?
Dealing with in-laws when you have kids

*The reason grandchildren and grandparents get along
so well is because they share a common enemy.*
--Sam Levenson

Chances are, if you have been married for more than 20 minutes, then your in-laws are already pressuring you to have a baby.

If your in-laws pester you too much about making them grandparents, here are some ways you can respond:

- Ignore them.
- Tell them you plan to get pregnant as soon as you conquer your cocaine addiction.
- Smile and tell them that every time they pressure you to start a family, it will delay the arrival of their grandchild by one year.

If you are debating whether or not to have children, then you're in luck because I have done extensive research[1] in order to provide you with information that may help you decide whether you're ready to (a) bring a new life into the world or (b) stop having sex completely.

---

[1] Mostly I just watched TV sitcoms or just made stuff up.

I don't mean to scare you, but your in-law problems (and therefore, your marriage problems) will likely get worse when you throw kids into the equation, unless you prepare yourself for what lies ahead. It's important that you learn how to minimize these potential problems before they start. In this chapter you'll learn how to claim your right to raise your own kids instead of letting your husband's parents call the shots. I will address these topics:

- In-laws who give unwanted advice about parenting
- In-laws who want to visit more often now that you have a child
- In-laws who compete with the other set of grandparents
- In-laws who undermine your authority

I will also offer some general tips about what to avoid so you don't invite trouble. And most importantly, I'll talk about how to motivate your husband to partner with you to raise your children.

IN-LAWS WHO GIVE TOO MUCH
ADVICE ABOUT PARENTING

From the moment your in-laws discover you are pregnant, they will have opinions about every single child-related subject on the face of the earth, starting with what you should name your baby. While they are making suggestions such as "Hilda" or "Walter," listen carefully while remembering to nod your head and smile. Write down the names they suggest. Let them know you appreciate their input and that you'll take it into consideration when *you and your husband* are deciding which name to pick. As soon as their car leaves your driveway, take the list and set it on fire. Don't even *try* to please them because you never will.

The two people who created the baby (you and your husband) are the two people who have the right to choose his[2] name. You also have a right to decide whether or not to breast feed him, pick him up when he cries, baptize him, discipline him, or enroll him in Pee Wee Football. It's your choice which pediatrician to take him to, when to start potty training, and when bedtime should be. You are entitled to choose what clothes he wears, and whether to put him in a private or public school. You have a right to decide which junk food he can eat, and whether or not he is allowed to eat on the couch. It's up to you to decide how much time he can spend watching TV and playing video games. And whether or not he is allowed to throw balls in the house. In other words, if a decision is to be made about your child, then you and your husband have an exclusive right and responsibility to make that decision because you are his parents.

This all seems very obvious, doesn't it? Sure, maybe it does to you and me. But unfortunately your in-laws probably don't think it's so obvious. And therefore your husband probably doesn't think it's obvious either. For some reason, things get twisted around inside of their heads

---

[2] For simplicity reasons, I'm going to keep using the pronoun "his" instead of "hers." It's not because I think boys are better than girls, so don't waste your time suing me.

and they end up thinking everything is a group decision when it is not. Your in-laws may think their opinions are just as important as your opinions, and in some cases they may even think their opinions are MORE important than yours. I'm not sure why some in-laws come to this ridiculous conclusion; perhaps it's because they consider themselves experts since they have already raised children whereas you have not. Regardless of why they feel they have a right to parent your kids, the simple fact is they *don't* have a right to parent your kids. You and your husband do. Don't let anyone try to convince you otherwise.

When your in-laws make a comment about how to raise your child and it makes you steaming mad, ask yourself why. Is it because you lack confidence in your ability to raise your child? If so, then find a way to stop allowing yourself to be concerned with what your in-laws think. If you aren't sure whether or not you should breastfeed your baby, then instead of remaining insecure and vulnerable, learn all you can about the subject from your doctor, books, and/or other mothers. Knowledge leads to confidence and that can make you less defensive about your in-laws' comments. Then the next time they say something, you can confidently agree or disagree without feeling threatened by them. Make sure you don't invite unwanted advice by bringing up subjects you don't want to discuss with them (for example, breastfeeding).

Make the most of opportunities early on to let them know you and your husband will make the parenting decisions, not them. If you truly believe that you and your husband have the right to raise your kids however you want to, then your confidence will speak volumes to your in-laws. The moment you start to doubt whether or not you have a right to raise your own child, your insecurity will invite your in-laws to butt in and take control. Here are some insecure ways for you to respond to your in-laws' advice:

- Get angry and defensive
- Cry, yell, cuss, storm off, call your in-laws bad names
- Complain to your husband about your in-laws
- Refuse to let your in-laws see your child
- Worry that you're a bad parent
- Assume their opinion is superior to yours
- Assume their opinion is fact

Be honest with yourself about why you are angry whenever your in-laws make a negative comment about your parenting. Could it be because you think what they are saying might be true? If your in-laws make a snotty remark about how much time your son spends playing video games, then evaluate whether or not they have a point. If you don't think he spends too much time playing video games, then don't worry about what they think. But if you do think he plays too many video games, then address the issue with him. Set aside your contempt for your in-laws in order to do what is best for your child; don't make parenting decisions just to spite your in-laws. If necessary, let your in-laws know you are handling the situation and that there's no need for them to bring it up again. Here are some confident ways to respond to your in-laws' advice:

- "Thanks for your suggestion, Harry, but I am going to do this instead."
- "You're entitled to your opinion, Helen."
- "I'm sorry you disagree, Helen, but this isn't your decision."
- "I know you're probably just trying to help, but when you make comments about how I should [dress / feed / bathe / discipline] Timmy, I get the impression you think I'm a bad parent. Is that your intention?"
- "I can tell by the way you are rolling your eyes (or shaking your head) that you don't approve of my parenting decision. Is there something you'd like to say to me, Harry?"
- "I'm willing to hear your suggestion if you can find a way to say it so it isn't condescending."
- "I know you won't approve of everything we do while raising Timmy, but we're going to do what we think is best. We'll probably make mistakes every now and then, but that's just part of being a parent."
- "You did a great job raising your children, Helen, but now it's time for us to raise ours."
- "I will probably be more receptive to your advice, Harry, if you wait to offer it after I have asked for it."
- "You may be right. I'll talk it over with Mike and we'll decide what to do."

Don't forget that *what* you say is just as important as *how* you say it. Be tactful; try not to be antagonistic or spiteful. Speak in a confident, clear tone. Make direct eye contact with your in-laws and address them by first name. Don't waste your time and energy trying to convince them that they should agree with you. Focus on letting them know it doesn't matter whether or not they agree because you and your husband are the parents, and therefore the two of you will make the parenting decisions. If you choose to ask for and follow the advice of your in-laws, then that is your decision. But you are not obligated in any way to do so, and the quicker you and your in-laws realize that, the better everyone will get along.

IN-LAWS WHO WANT TO VISIT MORE OFTEN NOW THAT YOU HAVE A CHILD

If you have already established boundaries about visits with your in-laws, then don't be surprised if your in-laws suddenly forget what those boundaries are. From the moment of conception, your in-laws will probably start wanting to visit their new grandchild constantly. But don't worry, you don't have to stop having boundaries just because your in-laws want to see your kid 24/7. It's important to set (or re-establish) boundaries before your child is even born. Seize every opportunity to create patterns that meet your needs. For example, before the day your newborn oozes into the world, decide as a couple who you want present (if anyone at all) at the hospital. You can take the grandparents' wishes into consideration but in the end, decide what is best for the two of you, not what will make them happy. You can decide when they'll arrive, how long they are welcome to stay, and whether or not they can sleep at your house. In case you care, studies[3] show that once a baby arrives, it's best for the hubby and wife to be alone with the baby (so they can bond as a new family and establish a routine) for one week before inviting either set of parents to visit. Let your parents and your husband's parents know in advance what you have decided and then be prepared for their reactions. If you anticipate that one set of parents might be jealous if the other set is invited to come sooner or stay longer, then it may be a good

---

[3] By "studies," I mean several of my friends gave me this advice. "Studies" also show that your in-laws (and maybe your own parents too) will probably hate this advice (but that's okay).

idea to address that issue up front and let them know how much it will mean to you if they make an effort not to compete with each other.

If your in-laws insist on getting together for frequent visits because they are "entitled" to see their grandchild, then let them know as tactfully as possible they aren't "entitled" to anything. You are still in the position to decide when you do and don't want to get together with your in-laws; having children doesn't take that right away from you. Here are some things you can say to draw boundaries about visits.

- "Helen, I know you want to come visit the kids today, but it's not a convenient time for us. How about if I drop the kids off at your house for a couple of hours on Friday evening?"
- "Harry, I'm really glad that you want to spend time with our child…and that he wants to spend time with you, but I'm not comfortable having you drop by unexpectedly. I need for you to call first to see if it's a convenient time for us to have visitors."

It might be tempting to use your child as a way to punish your in-laws since you don't care for them very much. You may want to refuse to let them have much contact with your kid simply because you don't like them. It's perfectly understandable for you to feel that way. However, it's not really fair to your in-laws, your husband, or your child. I encourage you to swallow your pride, be a mature adult and realize it's important for your kids to have a good relationship with their grandparents. (Make it a point not to criticize your in-laws within earshot of your child.) Unless your in-laws are abusive to your kid, don't stand in the way of their relationship. And remember, your child and your in-laws can visit with each other without you being there if that's what you prefer. You can drop him off for a visit while you and your hubby go on a date[4]. Or you can use the opportunity to run errands, go out with friends, or go visit your own family.

---

[4] Be sensitive to their feelings and make sure they don't feel you're using them as a free daycare center.

> If your in-laws tell your children negative things about you, then you (and your husband) need to have a serious talk with your in-laws. Let them know it is not okay for them to say anything negative about either of you to your children. If necessary, make the rule that they cannot be around your kids unless you and/or your husband are present. If they still don't take the hint, let them know you will severely limit their contact with your children until they stop this destructive behavior.

IN-LAWS WHO COMPETE WITH THE OTHER SET OF GRANDPARENTS

It's very frustrating to be caught in the middle of a war between your in-laws and your own parents. What are you supposed to do when they get jealous over which grandparents get to spend more time with the grandchildren? Are you supposed to act like nothing is wrong when they compete with each other for your children's love and attention? What are you supposed to say when they try to outdo each other by giving your children bigger and more expensive gifts?

Confront them about their unacceptable behavior and tell them how you expect them to behave from now on. You can say something like this:

> "Harry and Helen, we're so glad you love Timmy but we're concerned about the jealousy and competitiveness that seems to exist between both sets of grandparents. Obviously this isn't in Timmy's best interest, and it is uncomfortable for us as well. We have enough love for both sets of grandparents, and it would really help us if you could stop [buying so many gifts for] or [keeping track of which grandparents get to spend more time with] Timmy."

You can tell your in-laws you are concerned that your kids may become materialistic if they continue to send exorbitant gifts just to outdo the other grandparents. Encourage them to show their affection by sending small, thoughtful gifts instead of big, expensive ones. Or suggest they gain your kids' affection and respect by taking them fishing or to the park. If they insist on giving money, then ask them to donate to your child's college fund in a discreet manner.

Let them know that just because your kids spend Thanksgiving with one set of grandparents doesn't automatically mean that they will spend Christmas with the other set. Say that you expect for all of the grandparents to enjoy the time they do get with their grandkids instead of keeping track of whether or not they got their fair share. If necessary, determine consequences if either set of grandparents continues to compete for your children's time and attention.

IN-LAWS WHO UNDERMINE YOUR AUTHORITY

Do your in-laws frequently buy things for your child that you've told him he can't have? Do they buy your child toys that you've been encouraging him to save his allowance for? Do they say in front of your kids that they disagree with your punishment methods? Do they take your children to places without asking your permission first? Do they encourage your kids to break your rules and routines? Do they try to impose their religious beliefs on your child after you've asked them not to? Do they do things that constantly make you look like the bad guy in front of your kids? It's not okay for in-laws to undermine your authority.

It is possible they don't realize that they are offending you. Or maybe they do know they are offending you, but they don't know how to change. You can tell them how you want them to change. Here are some things you can say when you get the feeling they are trying to be the ones in charge:

- "I'm glad you want to spend time with Timmy, but from now on I need for you to ask me if it's okay before you take him to [see a rated 'R' movie]."
- "You have a generous heart and I appreciate that. I know you were trying to do something nice for Timmy by buying him that video game system, but we have been encouraging him to save his allowance for that. You had no way of knowing because I didn't think to tell you. In the future, I need for you to give me a heads up before you buy him something expensive like that."
- "I'd like for you to help me with something. I'm concerned that Timmy is getting too materialistic. Could you help me teach him the value of money by cutting back on buying so many expensive toys for him? I would sure appreciate your help and I know he'll continue to love you even if you don't show up with a toy for him every time you visit."
- "I'm sorry you don't approve of our punishment methods, Harry, but it's not your decision."
- "It's not okay for you to undermine my authority in front of the kids, Helen. From now on, when you have an opinion about my rules or punishment methods, I expect you to talk to me privately about it or keep your opinion to yourself."
- "Harry, I want you and Timmy to continue to spend time together, but if you undermine my authority by [doing this] again, I won't allow you to spend time alone with him anymore. None of us want that to happen, so I hope you'll decide to respect my needs."

Some of these boundary statements will be nearly impossible to enforce if your husband refuses to back you up. Be careful not to set boundaries you can't enforce by yourself. Later in this chapter I will give suggestions on how to get your husband to unite with you on parenting decisions.

> While some rules will apply regardless of where your child goes or whom he is with, prepare to be a bit flexible about rules at your in-laws' house. Rather than trying to set a rule about every single thing when your child is at his grandparents' house, teach him there are some rules that are different at their house than at yours. For instance, your grandparents may let him eat on the couch in the living room but that isn't allowed at your house. Or maybe he is allowed to run inside your house, but not when he is at Grandpa's house.

Realize that your in-laws are human beings and therefore they can't be perfect. Try to find a balance between flexibility and firmness. Overlook minor issues and set boundaries for major ones. Trust your instincts and be assertive when necessary. Have confidence in your own parenting abilities and don't take it personally if your in-laws don't approve of your decisions.

One of life's biggest challenges is partnering with your spouse to raise your kids. It can be frustrating when *you* want to raise your kids one way and *he* wants to raise your kids a different way. It's tough to figure out workable compromises when you have different opinions about rules, discipline, money issues, religion, etc. It can be extremely difficult to reach an agreement between the two of you, and it doesn't help matters when your husband's parents try to interfere. There are some things you can do to prevent your husband's folks from bullying their way into your parenting decisions. The most effective thing you can do is get your husband to realize that his role as a loyal husband is to partner with you – not his parents – in raising your children. Here are some suggestions on how to accomplish this.

Replace his false beliefs with truth. You learned earlier in this book that your husband sometimes acts like a bonehead because he has a bunch of unhealthy ideas stuck in his head. Your goal is to discover what those false beliefs are, and then try to get your husband to question them so he'll replace them with truth. The key is to speak to him in a gentle, loving tone as though you are really trying to understand him, which you are. Do not be antagonistic or judgmental. Here are some things you can say:

- "Honey, it seems that you think we have to get your parents' approval for all of our parenting decisions. Why do you think that?"

- "Honey, I'm concerned because it seems that you think your parents' opinions are fact. Is there some reason why you think your parents' opinions are more correct than mine (or yours)?"
- "Sweetheart, the neat thing about being grandparents is that all they have to do is love and enjoy our kids. It's not their job to guide and discipline them…that's our job. Is there a reason why you believe your folks should make our parenting decisions for us?"
- "Honey, I know your parents don't agree with some of the parenting decisions we make, but that's okay. They had a turn to raise their kids the way they wanted to, and now it's our turn to raise our kids the way we want to."

Communicate your feelings and needs. Instead of telling your husband that he and his parents are demons from hell, focus on how his behavior makes you feel. Tell him you need him to start behaving differently, and be specific about what you want him to say and do – or not say and do – from now on. Here are some examples of "I feel" and "I need" statements:

- "**I feel** betrayed when you make parenting decisions based on what your folks think instead of what you and I think as a couple. **I need** for you to stop discussing parenting issues with your folks and start discussing them with me instead."
- "**I feel** alone when you stand in silence after your parents have tried to undermine our authority. **I need** for you to back me up when I tell them not to [buy expensive gifts for the kids] or [criticize our parenting methods]."
- "**I feel** hurt when you listen to your parents say things to imply that I'm not a good mother. **I need** for you to tell your parents you think I'm a great mother, and that you aren't willing to listen to them gossip about me anymore."
- "**I feel** frustrated when you let your parents talk you out of a parenting decision we have agreed on as a couple. **I need** for you to stick to our decisions even when your parents disagree."
- "**I feel** unimportant when you encourage your parents to drop by unexpectedly whenever they want to see the kids. **I need** for you to back me up when I ask your parents to call first."

Suggest things for your husband to say to his parents. If your husband decides that he wants to start being a loyal husband when it comes to raising the kids, then he may need help figuring out how to put that into practice. Here are some things you can encourage him to say to his folks:

- "Mom and Dad, I know you're just trying to help but Jenna and I need for you to leave the parenting decisions to us."
- "Dad, I'm sorry you don't approve, but Jenna and I have decided to [put Timmy in public school]. It's not up for discussion."
- "Mom and Dad, I've listened to you make negative comments about Jenna's parenting decisions in the past and that was wrong of me. She is a great mother; she deserves my respect and yours. From now on if you have a problem with Jenna, I want you to discuss it with her directly instead of putting me in the middle."
- "Dad, it's not appropriate for you to criticize our parenting decisions, especially in front of the kids. If you do that again, we will either leave or ask you to leave."
- "Mom, if you continue to undermine our authority by [gossiping about us to our kids] or [taking them places without our permission], then we will stop allowing you to be alone with them."

For more ideas on how you and your husband can deal with in-laws who think it's their job to raise their grandkids, see the corresponding worksheets in the "Living as Friendly Vegetables" chapters.

Chapter 12

Help! I've Fallen...
Could You Bring Me My Roller Blades?
Dealing with elderly in-laws

The degree of one's emotion varies inversely with one's knowledge of the facts—the less you know the hotter you get.

--Bertrand Russell

One day when I was in junior high, my dad received a call from my grandpa. "I can't take care of Grandma anymore," he said, "I'm going to have to put her in a nursing home." So she came to live with us temporarily so we could evaluate what kind of care and attention she needed.

It didn't take long to realize we didn't have the knowledge, experience, or time needed to provide proper care for an elderly person. None of us knew anything about Alzheimer's disease. We didn't know how to make sure our house was safe for her. We didn't have an extra bedroom for her. The strain of having Grandma live with us quickly began to take a toll on my family. And although my dad felt a bit guilty for not keeping her at our house long-term, it soon became clear that it would be better for my grandma and us if she lived in a place where she could receive the professional care she needed.

It's common for many of us to feel an overwhelming sense of responsibility to take care of our parents when they lose the ability to take care of themselves. And that's not necessarily a bad thing. It's only a bad thing when we assume we are the only people who can take care of them instead of trying to recruit others to help. It's only a bad thing when we move our parents into our own home without considering other available options. Or when we refuse to take our own needs into consideration. Or when we refuse to value the needs of our spouse and our kids. Or when we assume our parents have lost their ability to take care of themselves when actually they have not.

If your husband's parents[1] are elderly and you are reading this book, then chances are that you, to quote Chevy Chase, "are standing on the threshold of hell." This chapter will address these three things: (1) how to determine whether your in-laws really need help or not, (2) dealing with in-laws who don't really need help, and (3) providing proper care for in-laws who really do need help.

---

[1] The information in this chapter can help you with your own elderly parents too...not just your in-laws.

DETERMINING WHETHER OR NOT
YOUR IN-LAWS REALLY NEED HELP

Your in-laws may or may not need help taking care of themselves. If they *don't* need help taking care of themselves, then it's important that you encourage them to be independent for as long as possible. Just because people get old doesn't necessarily mean they need help. And just because they ask for help doesn't necessarily mean they really need it. Some people pretend they need help just to manipulate others. For instance, if your elderly mother-in-law insists on moving in with you because she can't take care of herself, but then she invites you to go rollerblading, chances are she is a perfectly capable woman who is using her age as an excuse to get what she wants from you.

It can be difficult to have an accurate perception of whether or not your husband's parents need help. *You* may tend to think they don't need help with things because they are not your favorite people. *Your husband* may lean the other direction and assume they need help with things they don't really need help with because he is their son and he feels an obligation toward them. In order to get an accurate evaluation of your in-laws' needs, seek the non-biased opinions of experts in the field. These professionals can help evaluate your in-laws' abilities to see, hear, think, walk, drive, take medication, etc. While your husband may think the best solution is to move his parents into your house, a doctor may suggest that his folks stay in their own home and simply get a new eyeglass prescription or hearing aid. Talk to people who are experts in the field of elder care and ask them for suggestions on what you should and should not do for your in-laws[2].

It's important to find the truth about whether or not your in-laws really need help. It would be a bad thing if you and your husband *didn't* help his parents with things they really *did* need help with. And it would also be a bad thing if the two of you *did* help his parents with things they *did not* really need help with. Chances are that his parents do need help with some things and don't need help with other things.

---

[2] If your in-laws have a specific condition, call the corresponding organization such as the Alzheimer's Association.

DEALING WITH IN-LAWS WHO DON'T REALLY NEED HELP

It's important for your in-laws' health, and your own sanity, that you and your husband encourage them to be independent for as long as they are able to do so[3]. You may actually be doing what's best for them by refusing to help with something they are capable of doing themselves. They may get mad at you for not fussing over them, but that's okay. They may try to make you feel guilty for not revolving your life around them, but that doesn't mean that you are in the wrong. In the long run, it will be best for everyone involved if you and your spouse recognize his parents' ability to take care of themselves.

Don't make decisions for your elderly in-laws that they are capable of making themselves. If your husband's parents are still able to pay their own bills, then encourage them to continue doing so. If they aren't able to drive anymore, then don't assume the only option is to be their personal taxi driver. Encourage them to walk to the grocery store down the street if it is safe and comfortable for them to do so. Rather than visit your in-laws constantly because they are lonely or bored, encourage them to get together with peers to play cribbage, dominoes, bingo, etc. You could help them find a mall-walking group where they could meet new friends and get exercise at the same time. Or find a community daycare center that offers activities they enjoy. Keep persisting even if your in-laws show resistance; eventually they will probably be grateful for their improved social life.

Instead of moving your in-laws into your home, learn how to safe-proof their home so that they can stay there if that is a viable option. For instance, you can paint each of your in-laws' stairs a different color so they can tell where one step ends and the next begins. And you can replace most of your in-laws' appliances with ones that have automatic shut-off timers. Eldercare 911: The Caregiver's Complete Handbook for Making Decisions by Susan Beerman and Judith Rappaport-Musson includes a section on how to make an elderly person's house safe.

One way to help you and your husband determine whether or not his parents really need help is to familiarize yourselves with the difference between healthy and unhealthy attitudes among the elderly.

---

[3] Chapter 24 of I'm OK, You're My Parents by Dale Atkins discusses how to deal with parents who manipulate you with health crises.

Here is a description of an elderly person with a healthy attitude.

> *He is grateful for help when he truly needs it but he tries to remain independent for as long as it is wise for him to do so. He makes an effort to have a positive outlook and he treats others in a kind manner. He doesn't like being a burden to other people, so he tries to take care of himself to the extent that he is capable of doing so. He is willing to try new things and change old habits if it is best for him and/or his caregivers. He has planned ahead for his financial, social, and medical needs. His love for other people (for example his son and daughter-in-law) isn't dependent upon how much they do for him. He chooses to age with grace and he tries to make the most of the time he has left.*

Here is a description of an elderly person with an unhealthy attitude[4].

> *He complains a lot about being old, lonely, and helpless. He demands that others take care of him and is grumpy most of the time. He manipulates others by asking for help when he is capable of doing things for himself. He exaggerates his ailments in order to get sympathy and attention from others. He refuses to change his schedule, lifestyle, habits, etc. even if it would be beneficial to himself and/or his caregivers. He accuses others (for example his son and daughter-in-law) of being disloyal and unloving if they don't cater to him. He chooses to be miserable and wants everyone else to be miserable too.*

It's important to draw boundaries instead of doing things for your in-laws that they should be doing for themselves. If your husband doesn't realize his parents are capable of doing some things for themselves, then you will probably need to set boundaries with him as well. Here are some things you can say to your husband:

- "I'm not willing to let your parents move in with us, but I am willing to help you safe- proof your parents' house."

---

[4] Sometimes elderly people have cognitive problems related to Alzheimer's, etc. that may give them less control over their attitude.

- "I'm not willing to go visit your parents everyday, but I am willing to check into what social activities are available for them in our community."
- "I'm not willing to be your mother's maid, but I am willing to help her find a reputable housekeeper to hire since she doesn't want to do her own cleaning anymore."

Here are some things you can say to his parents:

- "I'm not willing to do your grocery shopping for you, Helen, but I am willing to help you find a taxi service for rides to and from the store since you aren't able to drive anymore."
- "I'm not willing to have you move in with us, Harry, but I am willing to help you and your friends come up with a buddy system for checking on each other to make sure you are safe in your house."
- "I'm not willing to listen to you complain constantly about your ailments, Harry, but I am willing to take you to the doctor to find out if there is some medicine you can take for pain relief."

PROVIDING PROPER CARE FOR IN-LAWS
WHO REALLY DO NEED HELP

Your in-laws may need help with transportation, home repair, yard work, groceries, bathing, paying bills, shopping, cooking, going to the bathroom, walking, getting dressed, eating, etc. It can be overwhelming to think about all of the care they need…especially if you or your husband assumes you must provide all of the care yourselves. I have some encouraging news for you: you have options. To some extent, you and your husband can choose which things you want to help his folks with, and which things you want to delegate to others.

Your husband may confuse love with obligation…he may think that if he doesn't take care of his parents all by himself, then he is a bad or unloving son. He may insist on meeting their every need regardless of the toll it takes on himself, his wife, kids, and career. He may be so sure that it is his job to meet his parents' needs that he may argue with anyone (you, for instance) who suggests other available options. Or he may insist that you be the one to meet all of his parents' needs while he goes about life as usual. He may accuse you of being a lousy wife or selfish daughter-in-law if you say you are too tired or busy to continue taking care of his parents.

If I just described your situation, then it may help to know you have the ability to bring about positive change. You can do that by (1) evaluating whether or not you are the best caregiver for your in-laws, (2) determining the best place for your in-laws to live, (3) researching what resources are available, (4) determining your wants and needs, (5) getting help, and (6) drawing boundaries.

EVALUATING WHETHER OR NOT YOU ARE
THE BEST CAREGIVER FOR YOUR IN-LAWS

You have two choices. Either you and Hubby can take care of your in-laws by yourselves, or you can hire someone to help. Before you or your husband decide that you will be the primary caregivers for his parents, here are some important questions to ask yourselves before committing to such a huge responsibility.

- What is your motivation for wanting to be a primary caregiver? Love? Guilt?
- Is it possible for you to maintain your current obligations (for example, working full time or caring for your young children) *and* be your in-laws' primary caregivers?
- Are you willing to give up your career, social life, and free time in order to be your in-laws' primary caregivers?
- What sort of impact will caregiving have on your marriage, kids, and health?
- How long will your husband's parents require care?
- What sort of things do they need help with?
- What sort of changes are you, your husband, and your kids willing to make in order to be available to help your in-laws?
- Do you have the skills and expertise necessary to take proper care of an elderly person?
- Do your in-laws have any specific medical conditions (such as Alzheimer's) and if so, are you familiar with how to deal with those conditions?
- Are you aware of the elder care resources available to you?
- Do you have friends, family members, and/or neighbors who are willing to help you?
- To what extent are you and your in-laws able to afford professional services?
- What will you do if your in-laws' condition worsens?
- What will you do if you decide to be your in-laws' primary caregivers and then you realize the responsibility is more than you can handle?
- Where will your in-laws live?

DETERMINING THE BEST PLACE
FOR YOUR IN-LAWS TO LIVE

Before you and/or your husband decide where his parents should live, here are some important things to consider:

- Is it safe for your husband's parents to continue to live in their house the way it is[5]?
- Is it possible to safe-proof their house so they can continue to live in it?
- Would it make sense to hire a home care worker so your in-laws can continue to live in their own house?
- Does their current house require so much maintenance that it would make more sense for them to move elsewhere?
- Would it make sense for your husband's parents to live in an adult home[6] where they can maintain a level of independence while at the same time live in a safer environment, engage in planned activities, and meet new friends their own age?
- Would an assisted living facility or nursing home be a good option for your in-laws?
- Would your in-laws' social needs be met if they moved into your house? Or would they be alone most of the day while you're at work? Would they be less bored in an adult home that has planned social activities with people their own age?
- Is there room in your house for your in-laws (and their wheelchairs, walkers, special beds, special toilets, etc.)?
- Do you and/or your husband feel comfortable bathing his parents, helping them to the toilet, etc?
- Does everyone in the family think it's a good idea to move your husband's parents into your house?
- Are your in-laws controlling and manipulative? Do they come between you and your husband (or you and your kids)?

---

[5] Chapter 16 of <u>Eldercare 911: The Caregiver's Complete Handbook for Making Decisions</u> discusses how to evaluate whether or not it is safe for an elderly person to continue living independently in their own house.

[6] An adult home is different than a nursing home … it is like a college dorm for high functioning elderly folks, except that instead of bringing beer to parties, they bring Ensure.

- Have you asked for the advice of a geriatric care manager and/or your in-laws' physician about where your in-laws should live?

Before you assume you can't afford any other option than to move your in-laws into your house, consider the fact that some places charge according to what your parents can afford. Think about how much it will cost to move your parents into your own home…especially if you're considering adding on an extra room. Compare that to the expense of other care facilities. Find out if your husband's siblings are willing to help pay for their parents' living expenses and caregiving. Make an effort to take your in-laws' wishes into consideration, but at the same time realize they may not have the ability to make a wise decision. Balance their wishes with the needs of your family and then make the best choice possible. Don't be surprised if at first your in-laws reject the idea of moving into an adult home or assisted living facility. It takes time to settle into a new place and make new friends. Just because they may be unhappy about their new living arrangements now doesn't mean they will still be upset a few months from now.

RESEARCHING WHAT RESOURCES ARE AVAILABLE

It can be very helpful to research what resources are available to help you and your in-laws. Here are some resources that may be available to help you take care of your husband's parents:

- Your husband's siblings and relatives
- Community groups and churches
- Organizations such as Alzheimer's Association, the American Stroke Association, American Diabetes Association, American Heart Association, etc.
- Local hospital with volunteer services
- Grocery store with delivery service
- Housekeeping services
- Telephone and companion reassurance services
- Medical professionals, certified eldercare professionals, respite care professionals
- Geriatric care managers
- Paid homecare workers or home health aides
- Adult Day Care Centers or Senior Centers
- Escort services for the elderly
- Meals on Wheels

Here are some things they may be able to help your in-laws (or you) with:

- Transportation (to the doctor, store, pharmacy, beauty shop, etc.)
- Sitter services (so you can run errands or even go on vacation for a week)
- Yard maintenance and cleanup
- Housecleaning and laundry
- Paying bills
- Social activities
- Personal grooming, going to the bathroom
- Getting in and out of a bed, chair, etc.

I don't have space here to get into more detail, but you need more details. To get a clearer idea of which resources can help you with certain needs, read some books about eldercare such as Eldercare 911: The Caregiver's Complete Handbook for Making Decisions by Susan Beerman, M.S., M.S.W. and Judith Rappaport-Musson, CSA. (Chapter 5 of that book is devoted to long- distance caregiving, in case you are interested.) To find out about resources in your parents' locale, call the Eldercare Locator number 1-800-677-1116. You can also contact the Council on Aging or the Area Agency for Aging. Visit www.seniorhousing.net to learn about places your in-laws can live in any area of the country.

Don't miss out on getting help just because you don't think you or your in-laws can afford the service. Sometimes services are offered for free. Other times they are covered by health insurance. It's also fairly common to be charged on a sliding scale basis that is determined by your in-laws' ability to pay. There's no reason for you to assume that you have to take care of your in-laws without help from anyone else! By using the resources available to you, your in-laws will probably receive better care than if you were to try to do everything yourself. You will likely have a better relationship with your husband's parents if you don't feel resentful and exhausted because you are trying to take care of all of their needs by yourself. Minimize your stress so your caregiving duties don't destroy your relationships with your husband or kids. Consider your in-laws' needs and then decide what you do and don't want to help with. For your own mental health, rally others to help with things you don't want to do. Take everyone's needs into consideration, evaluate your options, and then make the best decision you can and stick to it even if others (including your in-laws or your husband's siblings) disapprove.

DETERMINING YOUR WANTS AND NEEDS

In order to determine your own wants and needs, start paying attention to what makes you feel angry, overwhelmed, frustrated, resentful, stressed out, physically sick, and/or exhausted. Get a sheet of paper and write down a list of specific things you need and want. For example, "I need help with laundry once a week" or "I want to get together with my girlfriends one evening each month" or "I need for someone else to be in charge of dinner on Fridays" or "I want to hire a housekeeper" or "I need to start working part-time instead of full-time."

GETTING HELP

Once you have determined your wants and needs and you have researched what resources are available to help you and your in-laws, it's time to start asking for and getting help. Be as specific as possible. Don't expect others to be able to read your mind. They can't help you if you don't tell them what you need. Ask for help in a kind, non-judgmental tone.

- "[Sister-in-law], your mom has a doctor appointment on Wednesday morning. Could you pick her up at our house at 8AM, stay with her during the appointment, and bring her back here when it's over? If not, would you please find a transportation service that can?"
- "[Son], I need help in making sure your grandparents are safe in their house. Would you be willing to call and check on them on Monday afternoons when you get home from school?"
- "[Husband], I need help taking care of your parents. Would you be willing to come with me to meet a geriatric manager who can assess their needs and let us know what resources are available?"
- "[Daughter], I need to find someone to spend time with your grandpa this afternoon. Would you be willing to go on a walk or read a book to him?"
- "[Husband], I need help this evening. Would you rather clean up the dishes or help your mother get ready for bed?"

DRAWING BOUNDARIES

Here are some things you can say to draw boundaries[7]:

- "I'm willing to be the primary caregiver for your parents, but in order for me to realistically do that, I need to quit my job (or start working part-time). I don't have time or energy to do both."
- "I'm willing to pay someone to do your parents' yard work and home repairs if you're willing to start spending your weekends with me and the kids."
- "I'm not willing to move closer to your parents, but I am willing to find a reputable geriatric manager to take care of their needs."
- "I'm willing to [do this for your parents this week] if you're willing to ask [your sister, our neighbor, your friend, your parents' friend] to [do this for them next week]."

Some people (your husband, his siblings, his parents, etc.) may think you are selfish and uncaring for drawing boundaries, but nothing could be further than the truth. You won't be able to provide proper care for your in-laws if you lack the time, energy, knowledge, and skills required. If you are so overwhelmed that you are unable to take care of your husband's parents out of love, then you aren't doing anyone any good by doing everything out of guilt. You won't be able to be a good wife, mother, or daughter-in-law if you are resentful and frustrated with all of your caregiving responsibilities. You and your husband can get through anything if you work together as partners to handle what life throws at you.

---

[7] For more examples of boundary statements, see the eldercare worksheet in the chapter entitled "Living as Friendly Vegetables Part I."

Chapter 13

Naked Women (A chapter for Hubby)
Understanding why your wife and parents
behave the way they do

My wife says I never listen to her.
At least I think that's what she said.
--Author Unknown

Close your eyes and try to remember what your wife looked like the day you married her. Was she glowing with inner and outer beauty? Was she singing, smiling and petting small, furry animals? Did she look something like this?

Well, she may have been like that *then*. But as you well know, she's not like that *now*-- at least not when she's around your parents. When she's around them, she turns into a devil woman who could star in her own horror movie. Right?

Dr. Jekyl and Mrs. Hyde

So why does your wife act so crazy when it comes to your parents? I'll try to explain. Let's say you're on a hike in the mountains taking in the crisp, clean air and beautiful scenery. All of a sudden you see a bear up ahead of you on the path. You try to remember what to do in case of a bear attack. You know you're not supposed to panic, but it's a little too late for that because you just wet your pants. You want to run away screaming, but it seems you've read that bears can run 75 miles per hour, and that's when they *aren't* defending their cubs[1]. So if you can't run away, then what? Maybe if you raise your arms, the bear will think you are pretty big, and he'll think he's too wimpy to challenge you. Yeah, that sounds like a good plan. No, wait. Didn't you also read that if you encounter a *grizzly* bear, he will be ticked off if you try to look bigger than him? Hmmm. Perhaps instead you should drop into a ball to show him you aren't a threat. That sounds good. Too late. The bear is charging you. Having forgotten rule #1 (don't panic) you run away, alternating between dropping into a ball, raising your arms, and wetting your pants.

This is how your wife feels around your parents. She is probably as intimidated by them as you would be by that bear. What you see as your parents' normal behavior may be very threatening to her. She doesn't know what to do and so she alternates between yelling at you, criticizing them, crying, and running away.

The "Make Yourself Look Bigger" Defense

---

[1] If they *are* defending their cubs, they can actually beam themselves on top of you instantly from up to 5 miles away.

The "Drop Into a Ball" Defense

As the newcomer to the group, your wife is in unfamiliar territory when she is around your family. She may be letting her feelings of insecurity get the best of her. She needs to be able to trust you to put her needs above your parents' needs. She needs to know you value her opinions even if your parents disagree with her. She needs to be able to count on you to behave like a confident, independent adult around your parents. She needs to know you care more about being a sensitive husband than a parent pleaser. Do these phrases sound familiar?

- "I don't feel like you're on my team."
- "I want to be #1 in your life."
- "You care more about what your parents want/need/think than what I want/need/think."
- "You are more concerned with your parents' happiness than mine."
- "You would do anything to avoid making your parents upset, but you don't seem to care when your actions make me upset."

If your wife says any of these things, then she is trying to tell you she needs you to transfer your loyalty from your parents to her. If she can't rest in the knowledge that she has your loyalty, then she will feel

176

threatened. She'll be on the defensive and she'll be afraid to let her guard down around your parents. She'll fight with them for your loyalty every chance she gets, and she shouldn't have to.

Now it's time to take a look at why your parents behave the way they do. Close your eyes and visualize your idea of a perfect parent. Okay, you can open your eyes now. If you pictured an orangutan mother, then you're right. That's because orangutan mothers seriously rock. When their babies are young and needy, orangutan moms focus completely on them. They feed them, carry them, play with them, protect them, and even buy them cool Elmo pajamas. But the thing that makes an orangutan mom really great is that when she senses it's time for her monkey kid to become independent, she pushes him away. By doing this, she encourages him to begin a life of his own, apart from her. She understands that the goal of parenting is to raise a child so one day he will become independent. She understands that she isn't supposed to stay in the parent role forever[2]. It may seem a bit cruel to think of a monkey mom pushing her kid away, but think of how silly it would be if she continued to take care of him well into his thirties? She'd be walking around feeding, playing with, protecting, and carrying a 400-pound orangutan.

Because orangutan moms are so great at encouraging their grown kids to have healthy independence, you'll never hear them say unhealthy, guilt-inducing statements like these:

---

[2] That's why you never see orangutan newlyweds in counseling.

- "Why don't you call more often?"
- "How dare you ask us not to call after 9PM! We're family."
- "Why didn't you answer the phone when I called?"
- "Why don't you come visit us more often?"
- "Why don't you invite us to your house more often?"
- "Why don't you want to be with us?"
- "Don't you want to spend the holidays with us?"

- "Your wife isn't thankful enough for gifts."
- "Your wife is rude and/or overly sensitive."
- "We're just teasing. You should toughen up."
- "You didn't get our gifts to us in time (but your brother did)."
- "You should take our advice because we are older and wiser than you."
- *"You should* [say / do / buy / think / wear / eat} that."
- *"You shouldn't* [say / do / buy / think / wear / eat} that."
- "We are morally superior to you because we are your parents."
- "You are selfish, disrespectful, and inconsiderate (because you have needs that conflict with ours)."
- "Your wife is selfish, disrespectful, and inconsiderate (because she won't meet our unrealistic expectations)."
- "Why won't your wife call us "Mom" and "Dad"? Doesn't she like us?"
- "What do you mean you want us to live in a senior apartment? If you were a good son you would let us move in with you."
- "We expect you to take care of us even if it means you have to neglect your [marriage / kids / yard / finances / schedule / health]."

- "We took care of you when you were young, so it's your obligation to take care of us now that we're older (even though we are still capable of doing many things for ourselves)."

Although you'll never hear a monkey mom say those things, you may have heard your own parents make those statements. Or maybe they make nonverbal statements which are more subtle but just as damaging. Perhaps they breathe loud sighs of disappointment to let you know that something you said or did upset them. Or they glare at you to let you know they disapprove of your behavior. Or they roll their eyes around at you to make you feel inferior. Maybe their actions show they believe they are still entitled to be involved in every aspect of your life. For instance, they drop by without calling first. Or they interfere with arguments and decisions that should be kept between you and your wife (for example, how to raise your child). Or they invade your personal space by going through your mail, rummaging through your fridge, or cleaning your house.

Just because your parents may do these things doesn't mean they are horrible people. Sometimes parents don't know their behavior is inappropriate. They probably don't realize that by smothering you, they are making it impossible to have a genuine, sincere adult relationship with you (or your wife). They probably don't see that by controlling you, they are causing you to do things out of guilt and obligation instead of love. Maybe it's because their own parents were controlling and manipulative, and so they never had anyone model healthy parenting. Or maybe traumatic events from their past (such as the loss of a parent at a young age) have made it more difficult for them to let go of their role as your parent. Perhaps they *do* realize their behavior is inappropriate but for some reason they have a difficult time doing the right thing and instead they do whatever it takes to keep you dependent on them even if it means ruining your marriage.

You have probably heard a verse[3] that says, "Train up a child in the way he should go, and when he is old he will not depart from it." That

---

[3] Proverbs 22:6

implies that parents are supposed to let go of their role as parents. Otherwise it would've been written: "Train up a child in the way he should go and then follow him around for the rest of his life telling him what he should and shouldn't do."

Parents who understand that it's important to encourage their grown son to live an independent life will say things like this:

- "We love getting together with you, but we don't expect you to revolve your lives around us."
- "We know you love us even if you don't call and/or visit us constantly."
- "We'll be glad to keep our calls before 9PM if that's what you and your wife prefer."
- "You and your wife sure do a great job raising your kids."
- "We're happy to give you advice when you ask for it, but ultimately it's your decision."
- "You don't need our approval. Just do what you think is best."
- "We don't expect for you to share private details of your life (such as your finances or your sex life) with us."
- "It has been an adjustment not having you around as often, but we have made some new friends and discovered some hobbies we love."
- "We don't ever want to come between you and your wife. It's important that you put her feelings and needs above ours. Your loyalty belongs with her now."
- "We sure are glad you married Jenna. It's obvious she loves you, and she does a great job making your house a home."
- "We are getting older now and we don't want to become such a burden that you have to neglect your [wife / kids / yard / finances / health] in order to take care of us. Let's brainstorm how to get our needs met without having to depend on you for everything."

If your folks were evaluated by the Organization Of Parenting Skills[4] (OOPS), how well do you think they would rate at encouraging you to be independent? Would they get a high score because they value your opinions, or would they get a low score because they insist they are

---

[4] I'm pretty sure this organization doesn't exist.

always right? Would they get a high score because they realize your needs are important, or would they get a low score because they expect you to revolve your life around them? Would they get a high score because they encourage you to put your wife's needs first, or would they get a low score because they try to make you feel guilty when you don't make their needs a priority?

It may be difficult for you to have an accurate view of your parents because they are your definition of normal. You have been influenced by their beliefs and behaviors since you were born. If, on every day of your life, your dad had woken up and painted your eyelids green, then you would have grown up thinking it was normal for dads to paint their kids' eyelids green. If your wife grew up with a father who glued lifesavers to her head each morning, then she would think it was normal for dads to glue lifesavers to their kids' heads. Suppose you and your wife got married and had kids. Every morning you would fight about whether you should paint their eyelids green or glue lifesavers to their heads. My point is that you may think your parents have healthy, normal behavior but chances are, your perception of your folks might be a little off. It may be extremely difficult for you to realize that your parents try to control you with guilt whenever you behave like an independent adult or loyal husband. But just because you don't realize it doesn't mean it's not happening. You cannot become an independent adult or loyal husband until you admit that your parents' behavior (and your own behavior) isn't perfect. I've written a little test to help you evaluate whether or not your parents have healthy behavior.

Here are ten scenarios and typical responses from parents. Read through them and indicate which response your parents would most likely have.

Scenario #1: *You invite your folks to your house for Thanksgiving.*

- "No, we always have Thanksgiving at our house and we're already very excited to have you here." *(Inappropriate response)*

- "It might be fun to do something a little different this year. Thanks for the invitation." *(Appropriate response)*

Scenario #2: *You tell your parents you won't be able to spend Christmas with them this year.*

- "Don't you love us anymore? You can't do this to us. What could you possibly be doing that's more important than being with us? Holidays should be spent with family. We'll be lonely." *(Inappropriate response)*
- "We'll miss you, but we don't expect you to spend Christmas with us every year. You've got your own family now. Maybe we'll use this opportunity to take that holiday cruise we've always wanted to take." *(Appropriate response)*

Scenario #3: *You call them to say hello.*

- "It's about time you called. We were beginning to wonder if you even remembered that we existed." *(Inappropriate response)*
- "It's great to hear from you! How are you? We're so glad you called!" *(Appropriate response)*

Scenario #4: *They say they want to visit you on a certain day and you say that day won't work for you.*

- "Well, we're going to come visit you anyway. After all, we are your parents so we've earned the right to see you whenever we want to. Now stop being so rude and start being happy to see us." *(Inappropriate response)*
- "No problem, we understand you have other commitments. Just let us know another time that would work better for you. We look forward to seeing you!" *(Appropriate response)*

Scenario #5: *You tell your parents that you love them and will still make time to visit them sometimes, but that you won't be coming to their house every Sunday anymore.*

- "I suppose your wife put you up to this. It's obvious you want to spend more time with *her* than your own parents. Kids are so selfish these days." (*Inappropriate response*)
- "We'll be glad for you to come whenever you can make it. We know you and your wife don't get a lot of time off from work and sometimes there are other things you'd like to do." (*Appropriate response*)

Scenario #6: *You tell them you spent the day [skiing / playing video games, etc.].*

- "That sounds like a waste of time and money." (*Inappropriate response*)
- "It sounds like you had a fun day!" (*Appropriate response*)

Scenario #7: *You tell them that you just saw a particular movie.*

- "I heard that movie has bad language and sex scenes. You shouldn't be watching that kind of filth. Shame on you!" (*Inappropriate response*)
- "How did you like it? We saw a movie last night and it was great!" (*Appropriate response*)

Scenario #8: *You say you just had a Super Bowl party with friends.*

- "Why didn't you invite us?" (*Inappropriate response*)
- "That sounds like great fun! We just had some friends over to watch the game here, too." (*Appropriate response*)

Scenario #9: *You tell your folks you just got a promotion.*

- "How much money do you make now?" (*Inappropriate response*)
- "Congratulations! We're so proud of you!" (*Appropriate response*)

Scenario #10: *Your parents ask you to come fix their computer tonight and you tell them you'll come this weekend instead because your wife needs your help tonight.*

- "But we need for you to fix it tonight…can't your wife do without you for one evening? We have done so much for you. Is this how you are going to repay us?" *(Inappropriate response)*
- "This weekend will be just fine. Thanks for being willing to help us. Have a nice evening and tell Jenna hello for us." *(Appropriate response)*

Good job, you finished the "test." So what do you think? Do your parents generally respond in appropriate ways? If so, then that's great! If not, then you'll be glad to know there are some things you can say and do to bring out the best in them. By changing *your* behavior you can start having a more genuine, adult relationship with your parents. And at no extra charge you can strengthen your marriage at the same time. Oh, I almost forgot to show you a picture of naked women. After all, that's why you agreed to read this chapter, isn't it?

Chapter 14

Illegal Crack (A chapter for Hubby)
Improving your behavior toward your wife and parents

*I don't know the key to success, but the key
to failure is trying to please everybody.*
--Bill Cosby

Can you identify with this guy?

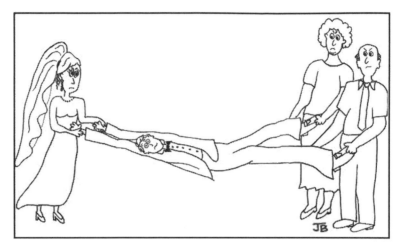

Groom Tug-O'-War

I thought so. Let me guess... it seems that no matter what you say or do, somebody is always upset. Either your wife is yelling or your mom is crying. Your wife and your parents don't get along. Your wife complains to you about your parents, and your parents complain to you about your wife. When you try to please one person, the other person gets upset. You feel guilty no matter what you do. Somebody is usually giving you the silent treatment. Nobody is ever happy (including you). And your sex life stinks.

TOP 3 WAYS TO SCREW UP YOUR SEX LIFE

1. Try to divide your loyalty between your parents and your wife.
2. Try to divide your loyalty between your parents and your wife.
3. Try to divide your loyalty between your parents and your wife.

If you don't enjoy being caught in the middle between your parents and your wife, then here's what you need to do: don't let yourself be caught in the middle anymore! You need to decide which team you are on. Let me explain.

When you were a little boy, your loyalty belonged to your parents. In other words, you were all on the same team and wore imaginary matching jerseys[1].

Then you got married, and since then you haven't been sure where to put your loyalty. That's the problem. On your wedding day, you were supposed to leave your parents' team and form a new team with your wife. You weren't supposed to take off your old jersey and put on a referee shirt.

Instead, you were supposed to take off your old jersey and put on a new one…one that clearly showed that your loyalty had changed and that you were on your wife's team from that point on.

---

[1] "Illegal Crack" is a real referee call, in case you didn't know. I'm a little disappointed it has nothing to do with a player's butt crack, because that would have been funny.

"A man shall divide his loyalty between his parents and his wife."
No wait, that's not how the verse[2] goes. It says, "A man shall *leave his
father and mother* and shall be joined to his wife." When a man marries,
it means he should start making his wife a priority over his parents *even if
that upsets them.*

Don't worry, when I say you need to place your loyalty with your
wife, that doesn't mean you have to stop loving your parents or start
being mean to them. It doesn't mean you have to agree with everything
your wife thinks or do everything she wants. You can still disagree with
her. You can still have your own opinions. You can still refuse to eat
broccoli. Being loyal to your wife doesn't mean you should ignore your
own feelings, opinions, wants, and needs.

Being loyal to your wife means you value her opinions even if you
disagree with them. It means you are concerned about her feelings. It
means you make her needs a priority over your parents' needs. It means
speaking honestly with your parents about your needs as a couple.

Whenever a situation comes up where you feel torn between trying to
please your wife or your parents, here are things you can say to your wife
to show her you are trying to be a loyal husband.

---

[2] Ephesians 5:31

GOOD THINGS TO SAY TO YOUR WIFE

- "I want to support you, but I'm not sure how to do that. Please tell me."
- "I know my parents aren't perfect."
- "I'm sorry you're upset, Honey. How can I help?"
- "Your needs are important to me."
- "You are my first priority and I love you."
- "Let's try to figure out a compromise we can both live with."
- "Can you help me figure out a tactful way to tell my parents what we've decided?"

Here are some statements you should AVOID during an argument with your wife because it will (1) communicate that you are not a loyal husband and therefore (2) decrease your chances of getting to sleep with her. In fact, if you ever hear yourself saying any of these things, go to your closet. Get a shoe and cram it into your mouth until you come to your senses.

BAD THINGS TO SAY TO YOUR WIFE

- "I don't think we should do anything that will upset my parents."
- "I don't have the courage to say 'no' to my parents so I'm saying 'no' to you instead."
- "My family has always done things a certain way, so we must keep doing everything that way."
- "We owe it to my parents to do what they want because they have done so much for us."
- "My parents' behavior is perfectly fine. You're the one with the problem."
- "You're [selfish / inconsiderate / disrespectful / too sensitive / paranoid]."
- "Let's not do that because my parents think it's a bad idea. I need their approval."
- "We should listen to my parents because they are older and wiser than us."

- "I have to call and visit my parents all the time because otherwise they will be lonely."

Not only do you need to learn what to say and *not* say to your wife, you also need to learn what to say and not say to your parents. The following statements are things you should NOT say to your parents because it would show you are (1) a little kid, (2) a disloyal husband, and (3) wimpier than George Mc Fly[3]. If you ever hear yourself saying (or even thinking) these things, stop what you are doing and go out to the garage. Get a hammer and smack yourself on the head. That should help you remember NOT to say (or let your actions imply) these things to your parents:

BAD THINGS TO SAY (OR IMPLY) TO YOUR PARENTS

- "Your needs are more important to me than my wife's needs." (If you insist on letting your parents determine where you should spend Christmas or how to raise your kids, then you are implying that their needs are more important than your wife's needs.)
- "It's my responsibility to keep you happy even if it means upsetting my wife."
- "I won't make a decision if you don't approve."
- "I choose to remain dependent on you for the rest of my life (even if it ruins my marriage and my life) because it upsets you whenever I show healthy signs of independence."
- "I'm willing to let you invade our space because you are 'family.'"
- "I'm willing to listen to you criticize my wife."

Here are some things that would be good for you to say instead[4]. These statements communicate that you are (1) an adult, (2) a loyal husband, and (3) a loving son[5].

---

[3] George Mc Fly is the geek from the movie *Back to the Future* who lets Biff bully him around, remember?
[4] For more suggestions on what to say to your parents, see chapter 13 of I'm OK, You're My Parents by Dale Atkins, Ph.D.

GOOD THINGS TO SAY TO YOUR PARENTS

- "Thanks for the invitation. I'll check with my wife and let you know what we decide."
- "Sorry, Mom, we have other plans for tonight. How about next week instead?"
- "I'm not willing to be caught in the middle anymore. From now on, when you have a problem with my wife, I need for you to talk to her directly."
- "I guess we'll just have to agree to disagree."
- "I know you're just trying to help, but this is my (and/or my wife's) decision."
- "Mom and Dad, you did a great job raising me but your role as parents is over. I need for you to be my friends from now on."
- "I don't tell you how to spend your money or time, and I need for you to show me the same respect."
- "I know you won't approve of everything we do while we raise Timmy, but we are his parents and therefore we'll be the ones making the decisions."
- "I'd rather not answer that question (about my finances, sex life, etc.)."
- "That is classified information. I could tell you, but then I'd have to kill you."
- "We've decided not to continue the tradition of meeting you every Sunday for brunch, but how would you and Dad like to go see a movie with us next Saturday night?"
- "We can have a close relationship even if we aren't in constant contact with each other."
- "Mom, instead of giving me a deep sigh on the phone when I say I can't come visit you, I'd appreciate it if you'd just say you understand and look forward to seeing me when I'm available."
- "I'm going to start calling and visiting you when I want to, instead of when I feel obligated."
- "Mom and Dad, we need for you to call first (or wait for an invitation) before dropping by for a visit."

---

[5] These statements may not seem to you like what a loving son would say, but the truth is that being honest and sincere with your parents is more loving than hiding the truth and having a superficial relationship with them.

- "Mom, I'm not willing to be your entire social life anymore. The community center is offering some classes for women your age…maybe you could learn a new hobby and meet some new friends."
- "Dad, I know you want to move in with us (since you are elderly), but that isn't a workable solution for us. Let's talk about some of the other options available, such as a senior apartment, home health aide, or meal delivery service."

Are you wondering about the verse[6] in the Bible that says "Children, obey you're your parents..."? Sure, it's a great verse for kids, but you aren't a kid. Your days of having to obey your parents are over. It's important that you and your parents treat each other as adult friends now. They aren't required to obey you and you aren't required to obey them.

Instead of obeying your parents, try applying the verse[7] about "speaking the truth in love." Rather than try to keep them happy at all costs, speak the truth about your needs and your wife's needs. Let them know when their behavior is destructive to your marriage.

And what about the verse that says "Honor your father and mother[8]"? You are NOT dishonoring your parents when you let them know that your wife's needs take priority over theirs. For example, just because you tell your parents you need for them to call before dropping by doesn't mean that you are dishonoring them. It's just as important for your parents to honor your needs as it is for you to honor theirs. I can't think of a better way to honor your parents than to have the courage to be more honest with them about your needs as a couple.

And don't forget about the verse that encourages husbands to honor their wives[9]. You can honor your wife by acknowledging that problems exist between the way you and your parents communicate instead of pretending that everything is fine. You aren't honoring your wife when you warn her not to rock the boat because you're worried that her honesty will upset your parents. You can honor your wife by doing whatever it takes to work out the problems between the two of you. You are honoring your wife right now by reading this chapter.

Changing your behavior toward your parents doesn't mean you have to have a big, scary, formal confrontation with them. For instance, if you and your wife decide you aren't going to continue the tradition of spending every Christmas at your parents' house, you don't have to call a family conference and give a 30 minute speech about how you've decided to transfer your loyalty to your wife. All you have to do is call your parents and say, "We've decided to spend Christmas with our friends in Colorado this year." Then change the subject. Try to be as nonchalant as possible and maybe they won't make a big deal about it if

---

[6] Ephesians 6:1
[7] Ephesians 4:15
[8] Ephesians 6:2
[9] I Peter 3:7

you don't. If you start to get a bad feeling in the pit of your stomach at the thought of being honest with your parents about your needs or your wife's needs, it may be because you've got some false beliefs stuck inside your head. Whenever you start to think you are an unloving, disrespectful son just because your needs conflict with your parents' needs, read the following statements to help you figure out the difference between the truth and heaping loads of poop.

TRUE VS. FALSE THINGS TO SAY TO YOURSELF

Load of poop: A good son never disappoints his parents or hurts their feelings.
Truth: If I want to be a loyal husband and an independent adult, that means sometimes my decisions will disappoint my parents and that's okay.

Load of poop: My parents' behavior is perfect 100% of the time and therefore anyone (such as my wife) who says their behavior is flawed must be wrong.
Truth: If my wife thinks my parents have unhealthy behavior, she could be right because no one's behavior is perfect, not even my parents.

Load of poop: My parents' needs are more important than my wife's needs.
Truth: My role as a loyal husband is to make my wife's needs a priority over my parents' needs.

Load of poop: I should allow my parents to talk down to me and boss me around as if I were still a child.
Truth: My parents should let go of their role of parents and start treating me the way they treat their adult friends. My parents are not on a higher level than me; we are all adults on an equal level.

Load of poop: If I do something my parents don't approve of, then I must be wrong because they are always right.
Truth: Sometimes I do things my parents don't approve of and that doesn't mean they're right and I'm wrong. It just means we're different.

Load of poop: I need my parents to approve of everything I say, do, think, wear, eat, and/or buy. It's their job to tell me how I should and shouldn't spend my time and money.
Truth: I am now an adult and therefore I don't need for my parents to approve of everything that I say, do, think, wear, eat, and/or buy. It is no longer my parents' responsibility to correct and advise me about how I spend my time and money. Their opinions do not outrank mine.

Load of poop: A wise son should let his parents decide how he should raise his kids because they have more knowledge and experience.
Truth: My wife and I should raise our own kids the way we feel is best, regardless of whether or not my parents approve of our parenting decisions.

Load of poop: I have to follow all of my parents' traditions until I am old and gray.
Truth: I can decide as an adult whether I want to follow my parents' traditions or start my own.

Load of poop: If I don't want to spend as much time with my parents as they want to spend with me, then I am an unloving son. If my wife doesn't want to visit my parents frequently, then she is a rude daughter-in-law.
Truth: It's okay to desire less time with my parents than they want with us. My wife and I aren't rude or unloving just because we don't have the same needs and expectations as my parents. We can still have a close, loving relationship even if we don't call and visit them constantly.

Load of poop: I should always answer the phone when my parents call, even if it's not convenient, because it's rude to screen a call.
Truth: It's not rude to screen a phone call when I'd rather not answer the phone.

Load of poop: My parents have a right to visit us whenever they want to, whether they are invited or not.
Truth: My parents need to show us respect by waiting for an invitation (or calling before they drop by). They need to be courteous even though they are "family."

Load of poop: If my parents are unhappy, it's my responsibility to do whatever I can to make them happy.
Truth: My parents are responsible for their own happiness, and I'm responsible for my own happiness. It's not my job to keep them happy.

Load of poop: If my parents ask me to do something, then I should say yes immediately.
Truth: When my parents ask me to do something, I can say, "I'll think about that and get back to you." I can take time to think about whether or not I want to do what they asked, before giving them an answer.

Load of poop: I have to be available at all times because my parents depend on me.
Truth: My parents need to learn not to be entirely dependent on me; there are others (friends, family, professionals) who can help if there's something they aren't able to do for themselves.

Don't expect your parents (or your siblings[10]) to stand up and cheer when you start behaving like a loyal husband. Hold firm to your decision even it makes them sad or angry. Expect them to try to get you to back down and change your mind when you start behaving as an adult. Here are some negative responses your parents might have:

- "Don't talk to your mother like that."
- "You are being very [disrespectful / rude / selfish / inconsiderate]."
- "We are disappointed in you."
- "We went to all the trouble of raising you, and this is how you treat us?"
- "Don't you love us?"
- "You're making a poor decision."
- "Your wife is turning you against us. You should make our needs a priority over hers."

They may act shocked, shake their head in disgust, or roll their eyes around. They might criticize, blame, intimidate, bully, or make fun of

---

[10] Your siblings may be mad at you for hurting your parents' feelings. They may try to make you feel guilty and urge you to apologize. Hold your ground and realize that your behavior is healthy even if not everyone approves of it.

you. They might cry, yell, hang up on you, or walk out of the room. Or they may flatter you in order to persuade you to do what they want. It's important to anticipate negative reactions from them so you can be prepared with an appropriate response.

APPROPRIATE THINGS TO SAY IF
YOUR PARENTS HAVE A BAD REACTION

- "I'm sorry you don't approve, but I am still going to [do / buy / eat / wear] that."
- "I'm sorry you disagree, but we've made our decision."
- "I'm not willing to discuss this anymore. Let's talk about something else."
- "Your guilt trips aren't going to work on me anymore."
- "You have a right to your opinion."
- "Tell me what you are thinking instead of shaking your head in disgust."
- "It isn't okay for you to treat me (or my wife) like this. I hope you'll decide to change your behavior, because otherwise I will limit my contact with you."

APPROPRIATE THINGS TO DO IF
YOUR PARENTS HAVE A BAD REACTION

- Maintain a confident posture and tone of voice
- Let them know you won't tolerate unhealthy behavior from them anymore
- Tell them how you want them to behave in the future
- End the conversation when necessary
- Don't admit fault for anything that isn't your fault
- Don't let your fear or false sense of guilt paralyze you
- Don't act like a child or a victim
- Don't defend your behavior or give excuses
- Don't engage in arguments or explanations
- Don't back down
- Don't criticize your parents
- Don't accuse or blame your wife for anything

Now take a moment to visualize yourself being able to handle the worst possible reaction from your parents. If you stand your ground in a respectful, loving manner, then they will eventually back down and accept the reality that you aren't going to behave like a child anymore. It may take awhile, but sooner or later your parents will get used to the idea that you are an independent adult. Becoming an independent adult doesn't mean you stop having any contact with your parents[11]. It means you can admit they have flaws. It means you realize they are on an equal level with you. It means you can make decisions without their approval. It means you can handle it when they are disappointed with your behavior, instead of changing your behavior just to keep them happy. It means you can behave like an adult even when you feel guilty for doing so. (Time and persistence will help your guilty feelings decrease substantially—in other words if you feel guilty the first time you screen a call from your mom, keep screening her calls and eventually you will stop feeling guilty for doing so.) Becoming independent means you can take your own needs into consideration instead of revolving your life around their needs. It means you make your wife your main priority.

You must learn to let your parents be upset. If your mom is sad because you don't want to visit her every week, then let her be sad. If your dad is mad because you won't cancel a date with your wife in order to fix his car, then let him be mad. If they are disappointed because you won't spend Christmas with them this year, then let them be disappointed. If they accuse you of being selfish and disrespectful, then let them think you're selfish and disrespectful.

What they think isn't fact; it's simply their opinion. If you never let your parents feel hurt, sad, offended, angry, or disappointed, there's a good chance that you don't have your priorities in the correct order. In order to take care of your own wants and needs, sometimes you'll need to make decisions your parents will not approve of. In order to take care of your wife's needs, sometimes you'll have to behave in ways that your parents will not like. If you can't stand to let your parents down and, because of that you do whatever it takes to keep them happy, then you are stuck in the role of a child and you haven't learned what it means to be a loyal husband.

---

[11] However, in an extreme situation, you may have to severely limit contact with your parents for a certain amount of time if it's the only way to save your marriage.

The next time you and your wife are having an argument about your parents, stop and look in the mirror. If you're wearing the old jersey from when you were a kid, then take it off. Or if you're wearing a referee shirt, then take that off. Find your new jersey –one that matches your wife's—and wear that instead. Show your wife what a great husband you are going to be from now on. If tomorrow your wife says she doesn't feel like she's #1 in your life, then ask what you can do to show her nobody is more important to you than she is. If some day next week your wife starts crying because of something you or your parents did, hug her and say her feelings are important to you. The next time your parents ask you and your wife to do something, consider your wife's needs and make a decision as a team. The next time your parents make a subtle negative comment about your wife, admit it's happening and put a stop to it. The next time there is an important decision to be made (like which car to buy, how to discipline your child, or where to spend Christmas), discuss it with your wife and make her input a priority over your parents' input.

You have the ability to bring out the best or the worst in your wife. The next time she starts acting like a psycho devil woman, take a look at your own behavior and make sure your loyalty is where it should be. The next time you and your wife have a disagreement about your parents, ask yourself the following questions:

- Am I doing what my parents need without considering what my wife needs?
- Am I assuming my wife is wrong just because she doesn't see things the way my parents do?
- Am I taking my frustration with my parents out on my wife?
- How can I behave in a way that places my loyalty with my wife?

In this book I have written two chapters called "Living as Friendly Vegetables (Part I and II)." These chapters contain worksheets designed to help you and your wife work together as partners to come up with compromises. The worksheets should make it easier for you to figure out how to be a loyal husband.

Why should you choose to be loyal to your wife over your parents? Because it could improve your sex life!

TOP 3 WAYS TO IMPROVE YOUR SEX LIFE

#1 Make it clear to everyone that your loyalty
belongs to your wife, not your parents.
#2 Make it clear to everyone that your loyalty
belongs to your wife, not your parents.
#3 Make it clear to everyone that your loyalty
belongs to your wife, not your parents.

If your wife knows you are loyal to her, then she will probably be in a good mood, and everyone knows that women are more likely to have sex if they are in a good mood. If you can learn to make it clear to your wife (and your parents) that she is now #1 in your life, then you'll probably see her transform from being an angry, deranged witch to a lovable, sane woman who wants to sleep with you.

Chapter 15

Living as Friendly Vegetables (Part I)
Using worksheets to achieve compromises with your husband

What counts in making a happy marriage
is not so much how compatible you are,
but how you deal with incompatibility.
--Leo Nikolaevich Tolstoy

"Jenny and me was like peas and carrots." That's how Forrest Gump described the bond between him and the love of his life. Let's say you and your husband just had a fight about his parents. Now imagine that I walked up to you right then and asked you to describe the bond you share with each other. Would you say, "We are like peas and carrots"? Or would you say, "We are like liver and head cheese"? My point is, you and your husband may need to figure out a way to go back to being the pea and carrot you were when you first started dating.

The purpose of the next two chapters is to help you and your husband live together as friendly vegetables. If you were a vegetarian, then you would know vegetables often use worksheets to come up with fair compromises. If you don't believe me, go to your refrigerator and open the crisper drawer. If you lean in close, you will probably hear little voices saying things like "Lettuce review our relationship worksheets" or "These worksheets can't be beet." This chapter has worksheets for you to fill out. The next chapter has worksheets for your husband to fill out. These worksheets will help the two of you state your needs, consider each other's needs, and work together to come up with fair compromises. By filling out these worksheets as problem issues come up (or before they come up), you and Hubby will be better equipped to achieve fair solutions rather than fighting like wolverines[1]. Give peas a chance.

Special note: To download all of my worksheets in a more practical 8.5" x 11" size, please visit my website at www.WifeGuide.org.

---

[1] According to a nature website, a wolverine "makes a Tasmanian Devil look like a sissy." If your husband ever approaches you with a low growl, bared teeth, and raised hair on his back, then back away slowly and lock yourself in the bathroom. Slide a "compromise worksheet" to him under the door and wait until things simmer down.

Problem Issue # 1: <u>PHONE CALLS</u>

My name is _____ and I am the wife.

1. If I were Boss of the Universe, these are the rules I would make about phone calls:
   - ❏ We wouldn't answer calls from anyone before 8AM or after 9PM unless it was an emergency.
   - ❏ We would get Caller ID and screen calls that came at inconvenient times such as when we were eating dinner, giving the kids a bath, etc.
   - ❏ We wouldn't call his parents back immediately when they left a message.
   - ❏ My husband would call his parents every now and then whenever he wanted to talk to them instead of calling them every day out of obligation.
   - ❏ Other_____

2. If I decided to be Mrs. Loving Wife (instead of Boss of the Universe), I would consider some of the following compromises with my husband:
   - ❏ "I'm willing to stop complaining that your parents call too often if you're willing to stop yelling at me for screening their calls."
   - ❏ "I'm willing to stop being hateful to your parents on the phone if you're willing to get Caller ID so I can screen their calls when I'm not in the mood to talk to them."
   - ❏ "If you want to answer the phone when your parents call after 10PM, that's your decision, but I'm not willing to talk to them after that time."
   - ❏ "I'll stop complaining that your parents call at inconvenient times if you are willing to let the answering machine get it when they call while we're eating dinner, giving the kids a bath, sleeping, etc."
   - ❏ "I'd like for your parents to keep their calls before 9PM and you don't mind if they call until 11pm. Let's compromise and answer their calls until 10PM."

❏ "I'm willing to _____
if you're willing to _____."
(For example: I'm willing to <u>do your Saturday chores so you'll
have free time to go fishing with the guys</u> if you're willing to
<u>stop answering the phone when your parents call after 9pm.</u>)
❏ Other_____

Stop now and read your compromises aloud to each other. Negotiate
until you agree on a fair solution. Take breaks if you need to get your
emotions under control or you need to get a fresh perspective. Write the
agreed upon solution(s) here. _____
_____

Now discuss the next two questions until you can reach an agreement.

3. How will we communicate this decision to my husband's parents[2]?
   ❏ We'll start turning the ringer off at 10PM.
   ❏ My husband will tell my parents we need for them to call after
     9AM.
   ❏ We will use caller ID and/or an answering machine to screen
     calls at inconvenient times.
   ❏ Other_____

Stop now and anticipate as a couple how your husband's parents might
react to your new behavior. (For instance, your husband's mom might
say, "Are you trying to tell me when I can and can't talk to my own
son?")

4. Here's what we will do if my husband's parents have a negative
   reaction[3]:
   ❏ We will stand firm and respectfully repeat our needs to them
     without backing down even if they are disappointed, hurt, or
     angry.

---

[2] See the chapter entitled "Don't Stand So Close To Me" for ideas on specific sentences
to use with his parents.
[3] See the chapter entitled "We Don't Need No Stinking Boundaries" for ideas on
specific sentences to use with his parents.

- ❏ We will set boundaries even if they try to make us feel guilty, inconsiderate, selfish or unloving for having needs that conflict with theirs.
- ❏ We will chicken out and let them call the shots about phone calls.
- ❏ Other_____

Problem Issue #2: <u>VISITS AT OUR HOUSE</u>

My name is _____ and I am the wife.

1. If I were Boss of the Universe, these are the rules I would make about visits:
   - ❏ My in-laws would visit [once a month / twice a year].
   - ❏ My in-laws wouldn't stay for longer than [one day / one weekend / one week].
   - ❏ My in-laws would wait for an invitation instead of inviting themselves over or dropping by unexpectedly.
   - ❏ My in-laws would sleep [at a hotel / in the guest room].
   - ❏ Other_____

2. If I decided to be Mrs. Loving Wife (instead of Boss of the Universe), I would consider some of the following compromises[4] with my husband:
   - ❏ "You want your parents to come visit [once a week] and I'd rather have them visit [every other month]. How about if we compromise and invite them over [once a month]?"
   - ❏ "If you're willing to agree that your parents don't come visit next month, then I'm willing to be the one to tell them that another time would be more convenient."
   - ❏ "You want your parents to come over Saturday but I don't. How about if you stay here with them and I'll spend the day shopping?"
   - ❏ "I'm willing to invite your parents over this weekend if you're willing to take me on a date next weekend."
   - ❏ "It's not convenient for me to have your parents visit in October. How about if we invite them to come in March instead?"
   - ❏ "You want your parents to visit us for the whole weekend, but I'd prefer if they don't come at all. How about if we compromise and ask them to come spend Sunday with us."

---

[4] These compromises will vary depending on several factors such as how far away your husband's parents live, whether or not you have kids, your work schedule, etc.

❑ "I'm willing to _____
if you're willing to _____."
(For example: I'm willing to <u>make love to you when your parents
come to visit</u>[5] if you're willing to <u>tell them they must stay at a
hotel</u>.)

❑ Other_____

Stop now and read your compromises aloud to each other. Negotiate
until you agree on a fair solution. Take breaks if you need to get your
emotions under control or you need to get a fresh perspective. Write the
agreed upon solution(s) here. _____

_____

Now discuss the next two questions until you can reach an agreement.

3. How will we communicate this decision to my husband's parents?
   ❑ I will call his parents and respectfully tell them that it's not
   convenient for us to have them come visit [this weekend / next
   month / in July] but that they are invited to come [next weekend /
   next month / in December] instead.
   ❑ My husband will call his parents and tell them they are welcome
   to come visit in March, but we need for them to stay for just the
   weekend instead of the whole week.
   ❑ I will e-mail his parents and tell them that they are invited to
   come visit us next month but that we need for them to stay at a
   hotel.
   ❑ Other_____

Stop now and anticipate as a couple how your husband's parents might
react to your new behavior. (For instance, your husband's dad might say,
"Who do you think you are, telling us that we can only stay for two
days?")

---

[5] Just to clarify, it's okay to negotiate a win-win compromise with sex as the reward, but
it's not okay to withhold sex as punishment.

4. Here's what we will do if my husband's parents have a negative reaction[6]:

- ❏ We will stand firm and respectfully repeat our needs to them without backing down even if they are disappointed, hurt, or angry.
- ❏ We will set boundaries even if his parents try to make us feel guilty, inconsiderate, selfish, or unloving for having needs that conflict with theirs.
- ❏ If my husband's parents insist on being in charge of deciding how long they will stay or where they will sleep, then we will tell them they either need to comply with our requests or they are not welcome to come at all.
- ❏ We will chicken out and let them dictate when they will come to our house, how long they will stay, and where they will sleep.
- ❏ Other_____

---

[6] See the chapter entitled "We Don't Need No Stinking Boundaries" for ideas on specific sentences to use with his parents.

Problem Issue #3: MOVING

My name is _____ and I am the wife.

1. If I were Boss of the Universe, these are the rules I would make about moving:
   - ❏ We would live in [Idaho / New York / Colorado].
   - ❏ We would move at least [200 / 400 / 600] miles away from his parents.
   - ❏ We would go visit them [once / twice / three times] per year.
   - ❏ We would invite them to come visit us once per [month / year].
   - ❏ Other_____

2. If I decided to be Mrs. Loving Wife (instead of Boss of the Universe), I would consider some of the following compromises with my husband:
   - ❏ "I want to move to the opposite side of the country and you want to stay in the same city as your parents. How about if we compromise and move two hours away from them?"
   - ❏ "We've lived where you have wanted to live for the past [10 years]. Let's live where I want to live for the next [10 years]."
   - ❏ "I'm willing to visit your parents [a couple of times a year/once a month] if you're willing to move farther away from them."
   - ❏ "I'm willing to drop the subject of moving for 3 months if, during that time, you will (1) stop expecting us to visit your parents so often, (2) let them know it's not okay for them to drop by without an invitation, and (3) start making my needs a priority over theirs. After the trial run, we can evaluate whether or not we should move in order to strengthen our marriage."
   - ❏ "I'm willing to _____
     if you're willing to _____."
     (For example: I'm willing to buy you tickets to the Super Bowl if you're willing to move to Idaho."
   - ❏ Other_____

Stop now and read your compromises aloud to each other. Negotiate until you agree on a fair solution. Take breaks if you need to get your emotions under control or you need to get a fresh perspective. Write the agreed upon solution(s) here. _____

_____

Now discuss the next two questions until you can reach an agreement.

3. How will we communicate this decision to my husband's parents[7]?
   - ❑ My husband will call his parents and respectfully tell them that from now on we need for them to wait for an invitation instead of inviting themselves over.
   - ❑ We will stop visiting them [every week].
   - ❑ My husband will tell his parents we will consider moving farther away if they continue to insist on visiting us constantly and dropping by unexpectedly.
   - ❑ We will tell his parents we have decided to move.
   - ❑ Other_____

Stop now and anticipate as a couple how your husband's parents might react to your new behavior. (For instance, your husband's parents might say, "We would be terribly lonely if you moved away. How can you even consider doing that to us?")

4. Here's what we will do if my husband's parents have a negative reaction[8]:
   - ❑ We will stand firm and respectfully repeat our needs to them without backing down even if they are disappointed, hurt, or angry.
   - ❑ We will set boundaries even if they try to make us feel guilty, selfish, or unloving for having needs that conflict with theirs.
   - ❑ We will chicken out and let them dictate when they can visit us and where we should live.
   - ❑ Other_____

---

[7] See the chapter entitled "Don't Stand So Close To Me" for ideas on specific sentences to use with his parents.
[8] See the chapter entitled "We Don't Need No Stinking Boundaries" for ideas on specific sentences to use with his parents.

Problem Issue # 4: <u>VISITS AT THEIR HOUSE</u>

My name is _____ and I am the wife.

1. If I were Boss of the Universe, these are the rules I would make about visiting my husband's parents:
   - ❑ We would visit them [once per month / twice per year].
   - ❑ My in-laws would visit us, instead of expecting us to go visit them.
   - ❑ We would stay at a hotel (or with friends) instead of staying at his parents' house throughout the entire visit.
   - ❑ Other_____

2. If I decided to be Mrs. Loving Wife (instead of Boss of the Universe), I would consider some
   of the following compromises[9] with my husband:
   - ❑ "If you're willing to call off the trip, then I'm willing to be the one to tell your parents we can't visit them this month."
   - ❑ "I'll promise not to complain about having to visit your parents if you stop pressuring me to visit them more than once a [week / month / year]."
   - ❑ "You want to go visit your parents and I want to visit friends instead. How about if we stay at our friends' house and then stop in and visit your parents some of the time we're there?"
   - ❑ "You want to go visit your parents and I don't. How about if you go and I just stay here?"
   - ❑ "I get along better with your parents when I don't have to spend a long time with them. I'm willing to visit them if we go out and see a movie or hang out with friends some of the time we're there."
   - ❑ "I'm willing to _____ if you're willing to _____." (For example: I'm willing to <u>go visit your parents next weekend</u> if you're willing to <u>watch the kids this Saturday while I go to the spa</u>.)

---

[9] These compromises will vary depending on several factors such as how far away your husband's parents live, whether or not you have kids, your work schedule, etc.

❑   Other_____

Stop now and read your compromises aloud to each other. Negotiate until you agree on a fair solution. Take breaks if you need to get your emotions under control or you need to get a fresh perspective. Write the agreed upon solution(s) here. _____

_____

Now discuss the next two questions until you can reach an agreement.

3. How will we communicate this decision to my husband's parents[10]?
   ❑   I will call his parents and tell them we will come visit them for the weekend, not for the whole week.
   ❑   My husband will call his parents and tell them that we won't be able to visit them this time, but that they are welcome to come visit us instead.
   ❑   Other_____

Stop now and anticipate as a couple how your husband's parents might react to your new behavior. (For instance, your husband's parents might say, "Why don't you want to come visit us?")

4. Here's what we will do if my husband's parents have a negative reaction[11]:
   ❑   We will stand firm and respectfully repeat our needs to them without backing down even if they are disappointed, hurt, or angry.
   ❑   We will set boundaries even if they try to make us feel guilty, inconsiderate, selfish, or unloving for having needs that conflict with theirs.
   ❑   We will chicken out and let them dictate how often we should visit them and how long we should stay.
   ❑   Other_____

---

[10] See the chapter entitled "Don't Stand So Close To Me" for ideas on specific sentences to use with his parents.
[11] See the chapter entitled "We Don't Need No Stinking Boundaries" for ideas on specific sentences to use with his parents.

Problem Issue # 5: **HOLIDAYS**

My name is _____ and I am the wife.

1. If I were Boss of the Universe, these are the rules I would make about holidays:
   - ❑ My husband and I would decide as a couple where and with whom to spend holidays without worrying whether or not his parents approved.
   - ❑ My husband and I would try something new and creative for holidays instead of doing the same thing every year.
   - ❑ Other_____

2. If I decided to be Mrs. Loving Wife (instead of Boss of the Universe), I would consider some of the following compromises[12] with my husband:
   - ❑ "How about if we compromise and spend Christmas Eve at your parents' house, and Christmas day here with just the kids?"
   - ❑ "If you're willing to spend Thanksgiving with my parents, then I'm willing to be the one to tell your parents we won't be spending it with them this year."
   - ❑ "I'm not willing to spend Christmas with your parents, but I am willing to invite them here for Easter."
   - ❑ "You want to go visit your parents for Mother's Day, and I want them to come here instead. How about if we compromise and meet them somewhere in between?"
   - ❑ "I'm willing to spend the holidays with your parents, but only if we stay at a hotel or with friends."
   - ❑ "Let's make a list of all of the holidays during the year, and then barter and negotiate with each other until we decide where and with whom to spend them."

---

[12] These compromises will vary depending on several factors such as how far away your husband's parents live, whether or not you have kids, your work schedule, etc.

❏ "I'm willing to _____
if you're willing to _____."
(For example: I'm willing to <u>spend Christmas with your parents</u>
if you're willing to <u>read two chapters in this book: "Naked</u>
<u>Women" and "Illegal Crack."</u>)

❏ Other_____

Stop now and read your compromises aloud to each other. Negotiate
until you agree on a fair solution. Take breaks if you need to get your
emotions under control or you need to get a fresh perspective. Write the
agreed upon solution(s) here. _____

_____

Now discuss the next two questions until you can reach an agreement.

3. How will we communicate this decision to my husband's parents[13]?
   ❏ I will call his parents and respectfully tell them what we've
      decided to do for the holidays.
   ❏ My husband will e-mail his parents and tell them what we've
      decided to do for the holidays.
   ❏ We will tell his parents in person what we've decided to do for
      the holidays.
   ❏ Other_____

Stop now and anticipate as a couple how your husband's parents might
react to your new behavior. (For instance, your husband's dad might say,
"Son, it will devastate your mother if you don't come here for
Christmas.")

4. Here's what we will do if my husband's parents have a negative
   reaction[14]:
   ❏ We will stand firm and respectfully repeat our needs to them
      without backing down even if they are disappointed, hurt, or
      angry.

---

[13] See the chapter entitled "Don't Stand So Close To Me" for ideas on specific sentences
to use with his parents.
[14] See the chapter entitled "We Don't Need No Stinking Boundaries" for ideas on
specific sentences to use with his parents.

❑   We will set boundaries even if they try to make us feel guilty, inconsiderate, selfish, or unloving for having needs that conflict with theirs.

❑   We will chicken out and let them dictate how we should spend every holiday.

❑   Other_____

Problem Issue # 6: <u>VACATIONS</u>

My name is _____ and I am the wife.

1. If I were Boss of the Universe, these are the rules I would make about vacations:
   ❑ My husband and I would decide as a couple where to spend our vacation without worrying whether or not his parents approve.
   ❑ We would have the courage to be honest with his parents about where and with whom we want to spend our vacation.
   ❑ Other_____

2. If I decided to be Mrs. Loving Wife (instead of Boss of the Universe), I would consider some of the following compromises with my husband:
   ❑ "I want to spend our vacation with friends and you want to spend it with your parents. How about if we compromise and spend this year's vacation with friends, and next year's vacation with your parents?"
   ❑ "If you're willing to take me to Hawaii, then I'm willing to be the one to tell your parents we won't be spending our vacation with them this year."
   ❑ "I want to spend our vacation in Las Vegas and you want to spend it at your parents' house. How about if we invite your parents to Las Vegas?"
   ❑ "I want to spend my vacation at my parents' house and you want to spend it at your parents' house. How about if we spend our vacation separately…you go to your parents' house and I'll go to my parents' house?"
   ❑ "I'm willing to _____
   if you're willing to _____."
   (For example: I'm willing to <u>buy that big screen TV you've been wanting</u> if you're willing to <u>let me decide how to spend our vacation this year</u>."
   ❑ Other_____

218

Stop now and read your compromises aloud to each other. Negotiate until you agree on a fair solution. Take breaks if you need to get your emotions under control or you need to get a fresh perspective. Write the agreed upon solution(s) here. _____

_____

Now discuss the next two questions until you can reach an agreement.

3. How will we communicate this decision to my husband's parents[15]?
   - ❑ I will call his parents and respectfully tell them we've decided not to spend our vacation with them this year.
   - ❑ My husband and I will tell his parents in person that we plan to spend our vacation in Colorado with friends.
   - ❑ Other_____

Stop now and anticipate as a couple how your husband's parents might react to your new behavior. (For instance, your husband's mother might say, "It's awfully selfish of you to spend your vacation in Hawaii when you know we don't get to see you very often.")

4. Here's what we will do if my husband's parents have a negative reaction[16]:
   - ❑ We will stand firm and respectfully repeat our decision to them without backing down even if they are disappointed, hurt, or angry.
   - ❑ We will set boundaries even if they try to make us feel guilty, inconsiderate, selfish, or unloving for having needs that conflict with theirs.
   - ❑ We will chicken out and let them dictate where and with whom we should spend our vacations.
   - ❑ Other_____

---

[15] See the chapter entitled "Don't Stand So Close To Me" for ideas on specific sentences to use with his parents.

[16] See the chapter entitled "We Don't Need No Stinking Boundaries" for ideas on specific sentences to use with his parents.

Problem Issue # 7: <u>TRADITIONS</u>

My name is _____ and I am the wife.

1. If I were Boss of the Universe, these are the rules I would make about traditions:
   - ❑ We would get together with his parents when we wanted to, instead of feeling obligated to stick to a rigid routine.
   - ❑ If his parents invited us to do something we didn't want to do, then we would say, "Sorry but we can't make it this time."
   - ❑ We would allow his parents to dictate our schedule instead of being honest about our needs.
   - ❑ Other_____

2. If I decided to be Mrs. Loving Wife (instead of Boss of the Universe), I would consider some of the following compromises with my husband[17]:
   - ❑ "You want to go to your parents' house every [Sunday] to [eat lunch] and I would rather get together with them once in awhile, and vary the activity and place each time. How about if we compromise and get together with them once a month (not on a specific day), and sometimes do things like bowling or watching a movie at our house?"
   - ❑ "How about if you promise not to pressure me to get together with your parents every week, and I'll promise not to complain about it when we get together with them once a month?"
   - ❑ "I'll agree to get together with your parents sometimes if you start checking with me before you commit me to doing things with them I don't want to do."
   - ❑ Other_____

---

[17] These compromises will vary depending on several factors such as how far away your husband's parents live, whether or not you have kids, your work schedule, etc.

Stop now and read your compromises aloud to each other. Negotiate until you agree on a fair solution. Take breaks if you need to get your emotions under control or you need to get a fresh perspective. Write the agreed upon solution(s) here. _____

_____

Now discuss the next two questions until you can reach an agreement.

3. How will we communicate this decision to my husband's parents[18]?
   - ❏ I will call my husband's parents and respectfully tell them we won't be coming to their house on [Saturday] for [dinner] this week because we have other plans."
   - ❏ My husband will e-mail his folks and tell them we won't be able to play chess with them this Friday, and then invite them to a movie next Saturday.
   - ❏ Other_____

Stop now and anticipate as a couple how your husband's parents might react to your new behavior. (For instance, your husband's mom might say, "I don't see why you can't spare Sunday afternoons to have lunch with us anymore.")

4. Here's what we'll do if my husband's parents have a negative reaction[19]:
   - ❏ We will stand firm and respectfully repeat our needs to them without backing down even if they are disappointed, hurt, or angry.
   - ❏ We will set boundaries even if they try to make us feel guilty, inconsiderate, selfish, or unloving for having needs that conflict with theirs.
   - ❏ We will chicken out and let them dictate when and where we should get together and what activity we should do during that time.
   - ❏ Other_____

---

[18] See the chapter entitled "Don't Stand So Close To Me" for ideas on specific sentences to use with his parents.

[19] See the chapter entitled "We Don't Need No Stinking Boundaries" for ideas on specific sentences to use with his parents.

Problem Issue # 8: <u>ADVICE</u>

My name is _____ and I am the wife.

1. If I were Boss of the Universe, these are the rules I would make about advice from my in-laws:
   - ❏ My husband and I would make decisions as a couple without worrying whether or not his parents approve.
   - ❏ We would not discuss our finances or sex life with his parents.
   - ❏ Other_____

2. If I decided to be Mrs. Loving Wife (instead of Boss of the Universe), I would consider some
   of the following compromises with my husband:
   - ❏ "I'll stop saying your parents are too nosey if you stop giving them details about our [finances / sex life]."
   - ❏ "I'd like for us to make decisions as a couple based on input from experts, consumer reports, etc. instead of just taking your parents' advice. If you're willing to do that, then I'm willing to stop complaining that your parents give too much advice."
   - ❏ "I'll try to stop getting so furious when your parents give advice, if you stop pressuring me to take their advice."
   - ❏ Other_____

Stop now and read your compromises aloud to each other. Negotiate until you agree on a fair solution. Take breaks if you need to get your emotions under control or you need to get a fresh perspective. Write the agreed upon solution(s) here. _____
_____

Now discuss the next two questions until you can reach an agreement.

3. How will we communicate this decision to my husband's parents[20]?
   - ❏ When my in-laws offer too much advice we will say, "This is our decision as a couple."
   - ❏ We won't bring up subjects that invite advice from his parents. (For example, we won't tell them how much we spent on our vacation.)
   - ❏ When his parents ask us about something we want to keep private we will say, "We'd like to keep that information between the two of us."
   - ❏ Other_____

Stop now and anticipate as a couple how your husband's parents might react to your new behavior. (For instance, your husband's dad might say, "You're a fool not to take the advice of your older and wiser parents.")

4. Here's what we will do if my husband's parents have a negative reaction[21]:
   - ❏ We will stand firm and follow through on decisions we make as a couple even if they don't approve.
   - ❏ Other_____

---

[20] See the chapter entitled "Don't Stand So Close To Me" for ideas on specific sentences to use with his parents.

[21] See the chapter entitled "We Don't Need No Stinking Boundaries" for ideas on specific sentences to use with his parents.

Problem Issue # 9: **FINANCIAL INDEPENDENCE**

My name is _____ and I am the wife.

1. If I were Boss of the Universe, these are the rules I would make about
    financial independence:
    ❑   My husband and I would support ourselves by doing whatever
        was necessary, such as cutting back on our expenses, looking for
        a better paying job, getting a second job, working overtime, not
        buying things on credit, or choosing a less expensive
        house/apartment/car.
    ❑   We would pay his parents back what we owed them as soon as
        possible, and we wouldn't borrow money from them in the
        future.
    ❑   We wouldn't live with my husband's parents.
    ❑   We would respectfully decline gifts with strings attached.
    ❑   Other_____

2. If I decided to be Mrs. Loving Wife (instead of Boss of the Universe),
    I would consider some of the following compromises with my
    husband:
    ❑   "I want to find alternate daycare, and you want your parents to
        watch our kids every day. How about if your parents watch them
        one day a week and we'll put them in daycare on the other
        days?"
    ❑   "I'm willing to stop complaining about owing your parents
        money if you're willing to come with me to see a financial
        counselor."
    ❑   "I want to politely refuse your parents' gift and you want to
        accept it. How about if we tell them we will accept the gift as
        long as there are no strings attached?"

❑ "I'm willing to _____
   if you're willing to _____."
   (For example: I'm willing to <u>make love to you four times a week</u>
   <u>for a month</u>[22] if you're willing to <u>give your parents two weeks</u>
   <u>notice that you aren't going to work for them anymore</u>.)
❑ Other_____

Stop now and read your compromises aloud to each other. Negotiate
until you agree on a fair solution. Take breaks if you need to get your
emotions under control or you need to get a fresh perspective. Write the
agreed upon solution(s) here. _____

_____

Now discuss the next two questions until you can reach an agreement.

3. How will we communicate this decision to my husband's parents[23]?
   ❑ We will respectfully tell his parents we will be moving out of
      their house [next month].
   ❑ When my husband's parents give us a gift with strings attached, I
      will clarify their motives before accepting it.
   ❑ We will pay his parents the money we owe them; we will use a
      lending institute for future loans.
   ❑ My husband will call his parents and tell them we have decided
      to change our daycare arrangements.
   ❑ Other_____

Stop now and anticipate as a couple how your husband's parents might
react to your new behavior. (For instance, your husband's parents might
say, "You'll never make it on your own; just be grateful we are so
generous.")

---

[22] Just to clarify, it's okay to negotiate a win-win compromise with sex as the reward,
but it's not okay to withhold sex as punishment.
[23] See the chapter entitled "Don't Stand So Close To Me" for ideas on specific sentences
to use with his parents.

4. Here's what we will do if my husband's parents have a negative reaction[24]:

❑ We will stand firm and respectfully repeat our decisions to them without backing down even if they are disappointed, hurt, or angry.

❑ We will set boundaries even if they try to make us feel guilty, inconsiderate, rude, or ungrateful for wanting financial independence.

❑ We will chicken out and stay financially dependent on them even though we are capable adults.

❑ Other_____

---

[24] See the chapter entitled "We Don't Need No Stinking Boundaries" for ideas on specific sentences to use with his parents.

Problem Issue # 10: <u>CHILDREN</u>

My name is _____ and I am the wife.

1. If I were Boss of the Universe, these are the rules I would make about raising our kids:
   - ❑ My husband and I would make parenting decisions as a couple without worrying whether or not his parents approved.
   - ❑ We would not discuss our parenting decisions with his parents.
   - ❑ We would not tolerate it when his parents criticize our parenting skills or refuse to follow the rules we have for our kids.
   - ❑ We would insist his folks call first or wait for an invitation instead of just dropping by to see the kids.
   - ❑ We would confront his parents about competing with the other set of grandparents for our child's love and attention.
   - ❑ Other_____

2. If I decided to be Mrs. Loving Wife (instead of Boss of the Universe), I would consider some of the following compromises with my husband:
   - ❑ "I'm willing to stop saying your parents are too nosey if you're willing to start discussing parenting decisions with me instead of them."
   - ❑ "I'd like for us to make decisions as a couple based on input from books, magazines, and friends instead of just taking your parents' advice about everything. If you're willing to do that, then I'm willing to stop complaining that your parents give too much advice."
   - ❑ "I'm willing to let our son spend more time with your folks if you're willing to back me up when I [tell them to ask for our permission before taking him somewhere] or [tell them to stop buying him such expensive gifts]."
   - ❑ "I'm not willing to let your parents invite themselves over whenever they want to just because they want to see the grandkids. However, I am willing to drop the kids off to visit them next Friday if that is convenient for your parents."

❑ "I'm willing to be flexible about some rules when our kids are with your folks, but I'm not willing to be flexible about [their bedtime]."

❑ "I'm willing to invite your parents for a visit if you're willing to tell them we want them to stop competing with my parents for our children's love and attention."

❑ Other_____

Stop now and read your compromises aloud to each other. Negotiate until you agree on a fair solution. Take breaks if you need to get your emotions under control or you need to get a fresh perspective. Write the agreed upon solution(s) here. _____

_____

Now discuss the next two questions until you can reach an agreement.

3. How will we communicate this decision to my husband's parents[25]?

❑ When my husband's parents offer too much advice, we will say, "Thanks for your advice, but we've decided to do something else."

❑ I will tell them they must to call first or wait for an invitation instead of dropping by to see the kids whenever they want.

❑ Other_____

Stop now and anticipate as a couple how your husband's parents might react to your new behavior. (For instance, your husband's parents might say, "You would be wise to let us help you raise your kids since we have so much experience.")

4. Here's what we will do if my husband's parents have a negative reaction[26]:

❑ We will stand firm and follow through on our parenting decisions even if they don't approve, or they try to make us feel guilty, disrespectful, or foolish for not taking their advice.

---

[25] See the chapter entitled "How Many Forms of Birth Control Can I Safely Use at One Time?" for ideas on specific sentences to use with his parents.

[26] See the chapter entitled "We Don't Need No Stinking Boundaries" for ideas on specific sentences to use with his parents.

❑   We will restate our needs without backing down even if they get upset.
❑   We will let them decide how to raise our kids even though we are the parents.
❑   Other_____

Problem Issue # 11: ELDER CARE

My name is _____ and I am the wife.

1. If I were Boss of the Universe, these are the rules I would make about taking care of my husband's elderly parents:
   - ❑ My husband's parents would move to a [senior apartment / assisted living facility / nursing home].
   - ❑ My husband and I would seek the help of friends, relatives, and professionals in order to take care of his parents.
   - ❑ We would stop helping them with things they are capable of doing themselves.
   - ❑ Other_____

2. If I decided to be Mrs. Loving Wife (instead of Boss of the Universe), I would consider some of the following compromises with my husband:
   - ❑ "I'm willing to help your parents with transportation and meals, but I'm not willing to bathe them or help them go to the bathroom. Are you willing to do those things, or should we hire a professional?"
   - ❑ "I'm not willing to drive your father to all of his doctor appointments, but I am willing to pay a company to transport him in a van equipped for wheelchairs."
   - ❑ "I'm willing to do your dad's cooking and laundry if you're willing to pay his bills and entertain him for an hour each night."
   - ❑ "I'm not willing to be your parents' primary caregiver, but I am willing to find a reputable homecare worker who can give your parents the proper care they need."
   - ❑ "I'm willing to research how to make your parents' home safe for them if you're willing to stop insisting they move in with us."
   - ❑ "I'm not willing to let your parents come live with us, but I am willing to do some research to find an adult home or assisted living facility to help meet your parents' needs for safety, social activities, and well-balanced meals."
   - ❑ Other_____

Stop now and read your compromises aloud to each other. Negotiate until you agree on a fair solution. Take breaks if you need to get your emotions under control or you need to get a fresh perspective. Write the agreed upon solution(s) here. _____

_____

Now discuss the next two questions until you can reach an agreement.

3. How will we communicate this decision to my husband's parents[27]?
   - ❑ We will visit my husband's parents and ask them whether they would like to move into an assisted living facility or have a homecare worker come to their house.
   - ❑ I will call my mother-in-law and let her know I won't be available to drive her to the doctor on Friday and then ask whether she would prefer a friend, neighbor, relative, or taxi service to take her instead.
   - ❑ Other_____

Stop now and anticipate as a couple how your husband's parents might react to your new behavior. (For instance, your husband's mom might say, "I'll be so lonely if you don't let me move in with you.")

4. Here's what we will do if my husband's parents have a negative reaction[28]:
   - ❑ We will be respectful toward my husband's parents, but we will stand our ground even if they are disappointed, hurt, or angry.
   - ❑ We will hold strong to what we agreed upon even if they try to make us feel guilty, inconsiderate, selfish, or unloving for having needs that conflict with theirs.
   - ❑ We will cave under pressure and agree to all of their demands even if it destroys our marriage, health, and social life.
   - ❑ Other_____

---

[27] See the chapter entitled "Help I've Fallen…Could You Bring Me My Roller Blades?" for ideas on specific sentences to use with his parents.

[28] See the chapter entitled "We Don't Need No Stinking Boundaries" for ideas on specific sentences to use with his parents.

Chapter 16

Living as Friendly Vegetables (Part II)
Using worksheets to achieve compromises with your wife

People who work together will win,
whether it be against complex football
defenses, or the problems of modern society.
--Vince Lombardi

Problem Issue #1: <u>PHONE CALLS</u>

My name is _____ and I am the husband. I would rather go to the opera than fill out this worksheet, but I'm doing it anyway because I love my wife.

1. Whenever the topic of phone calls comes up, my wife says/does these things that make me want to buy her a bouquet of poison ivy:
   - ❑ She complains that my parents call too early, too late, and too often.
   - ❑ She screens their phone calls when she is too busy to talk to them.
   - ❑ She doesn't return my parents' phone calls immediately.
   - ❑ Other_____

2. If my parents were the bosses of the universe, these are the rules they would make about calls:
   - ❑ "Our son and his wife should answer the phone every time we call, even if they are busy eating dinner, bathing the kids, exercising, etc."
   - ❑ "Our son and daughter-in-law should cheerfully answer the phone regardless of what time of the morning or night we call, because we are family."
   - ❑ "Our son and his wife should never screen our calls, even if we call at inconvenient or inappropriate times."
   - ❑ Other_____

3. If I were Boss of the Universe, these are the rules I would make about phone calls:
   - ❑ My parents would only call once a week instead of everyday.
   - ❑ I would call my parents when I *wanted* to instead of when I thought I *should*.
   - ❑ My wife and I would answer the phone every single time the phone rings even if we are busy doing something else at the time.
   - ❑ I wouldn't answer phone calls while I was eating a meal, putting the kids to bed, entertaining friends, in the middle my favorite TV show, sleeping, having sex, or driving.

- ❏ My wife and I would answer my parents' phone calls at any time of morning or night regardless of our needs.
- ❏ My parents wouldn't call before 9AM or after 10PM.
- ❏ Other_____

4. If I decided to be Mr. Loving Husband (instead of Boss of the Universe), I would consider some of the following compromises with my wife:
   - ❏ "You don't like for my parents to call after 8PM, and I don't mind if they call until midnight. Let's compromise and start letting the answering machine get it whenever people call us after 10PM."
   - ❏ "I'm willing to start screening calls from my parents during dinner and after 10PM. In exchange, I'd like for you to be nicer when you talk to them on the phone."
   - ❏ "It's fine with me if you prefer that my parents keep their calls between 8AM and 8PM, but you will have to be the one to tell them."
   - ❏ Other_____

Stop now and read your compromises aloud to each other. Negotiate until you agree on a fair solution. Take breaks if you need to get your emotions under control or you need to get a fresh perspective. Write the agreed upon solutions here._____

_____

Now discuss the next two questions until you can reach an agreement.

5. How will we communicate this decision to my parents[1]?
   - ❏ We will use caller ID and/or an answering machine to screen calls at inconvenient times.
   - ❏ I'll call my parents when I want to talk to them, instead of calling them several times a week out of obligation.
   - ❏ Instead of returning my parents' calls immediately, sometimes we will wait until the next day, or e-mail them instead.
   - ❏ My wife will tell my parents we need for them to keep their calls before 10pm.

---

[1] See the chapter entitled "Illegal Crack" (the section called 'Good Things To Say To Your Parents') for ideas on specific sentences to use with your parents.

❑   I will tell my parents we need for them to stop calling before 8am in the morning.

❑   Other_____

Stop now and anticipate as a couple how your parents might react to your new behavior. (For instance, they might say, "I don't see why we can't call whenever we want to…we're family.")

6. Here's what we will do if my parents have a negative reaction[2]:

❑   I will be respectful and loving toward my parents, but I will stand firm and repeat our needs to them without backing down even if they are disappointed, hurt, or angry.

❑   We will chicken out and let them dictate when we should and shouldn't call them and/or answer their calls.

❑   Other_____

---

[2] See the chapter entitled "Illegal Crack" (the section called 'Appropriate Things To Say If Your Parents Have A Bad Reaction') for specific sentences to use with your parents.

Problem Issue #2: <u>VISITS AT OUR HOUSE</u>

My name is _____ and I am the husband. I would rather stick my head in a bucket of hot oil than fill out this worksheet, but I'm doing it anyway because I love my wife (even though she drives me crazy).

1. Whenever the topic of a visit from my parents comes up, my wife does these things that make me want to leave her in the desert with no water:
   - ❏ She says it's an inconvenient time to have my parents come visit.
   - ❏ She flies off the handle when my parents invite themselves over or show up unexpectedly on our doorstep.
   - ❏ She complains that my parents visit too often and too long.
   - ❏ She wants my parents to stay in the guest room (or a hotel) instead of our bedroom.
   - ❏ Other_____

2. If my parents were the bosses of the universe, these are the rules they would make about visiting our house:
   - ❏ "Our son and his wife should invite us to come visit them [every day / once a week / once a month] even if they would prefer to have us visit less often."
   - ❏ "Our son and daughter-in-law should welcome us into their home whenever we drop by unexpectedly, even if we show up at an inconvenient time."
   - ❏ "Our son and his wife should allow us to stay for at least [3 hours / 3 days / 3 weeks] when we come to visit, even if they would prefer our visits to be shorter."
   - ❏ Other_____

3. If I were Boss of the Universe, these are the rules I would make about visits:
   - ❏ My parents would come visit us [once a week / once a month / once a year] and stay for [one hour / one day / one week].
   - ❏ My parents would call first instead of just dropping by.

- ❏ If my parents invited themselves over at an inconvenient time, we would feel free to say, "Sorry but this isn't a good time for us."
- ❏ My wife and I would allow my parents to come visit us whenever they wanted to, regardless of our needs, because I think it's better to do things out of obligation than to be honest with them about our needs.
- ❏ My parents would stay in the guest room (or hotel) instead of our master bedroom when they came to visit.
- ❏ Other_____

4. If I decided to be Mr. Loving Husband (instead of Boss of the Universe), I would consider some of the following compromises[3] with my wife:

- ❏ "How about if I promise not to pressure you to invite my parents over more than [twice a year] if you promise not to complain about it when they come then."
- ❏ "We don't have to invite my parents here in [April] since it's not good timing for you, but how about if I invite them to come in [May]?"
- ❏ "I know you don't want my parents to stay for a whole week. How about if they stay for just the weekend?"
- ❏ "Since you don't want my parents to come to our house, what would you think of meeting them somewhere between our house and theirs?"
- ❏ "You don't like the idea of my parents coming to visit us next week, but how would you feel if I told them we needed for them to stay in a hotel?"
- ❏ "I'm willing to _____ if you're willing to _____." (For example: I'm willing to <u>do the cooking and the dishes every day for a week</u> if you're willing <u>to invite my parents to our house on my mom's birthday weekend.</u>")
- ❏ Other_____

Stop now and read your compromises aloud to each other. Negotiate until you agree on a fair solution. Take breaks if you need to get your

_____

[3] These compromises will vary depending on several factors such as how far away your parents live, whether or not you have kids, your work schedule, etc.

emotions under control or you need to get a fresh perspective. Write the agreed upon solution(s) here. _____

_____

Now discuss the next two questions until you can reach an agreement.

5. How will we communicate this decision to my parents[4]?
   - ❏ I will call my parents and respectfully tell them that it's not convenient for us to have them come visit [this weekend / next month] but that they are invited to come [next weekend / next month] instead.
   - ❏ My wife will call my parents and tell them they are welcome to come visit in November, but we need for them to stay for just the weekend instead of the whole week.
   - ❏ When my parents get to our house, I'll carry their luggage into the guest bedroom instead of our room.
   - ❏ Other_____

Stop now and anticipate as a couple how your parents might react to your new behavior. (For instance, your dad might say, "We've already decided when we are coming for a visit, so you're going to have to cancel your plans.")

6. Here's what we will do if my parents have a negative reaction[5]:
   - ❏ I will hold strong to what my wife and I agreed upon even if my parents try to make me feel guilty, inconsiderate, selfish, or unloving for having needs that conflict with theirs.
   - ❏ If my parents insist on being in charge of deciding how long they will stay or where they will sleep, etc., then we will tell them they either need to comply with our requests or they are not welcome to come at all[6].

_____

[4] See the chapter entitled "Illegal Crack" (the section called 'Good Things To Say To Your Parents') for ideas on specific sentences to use with your parents.
[5] See the chapter entitled "Illegal Crack" (the section called 'Appropriate Things To Say If Your Parents Have A Bad Reaction') for specific sentences to use with your parents.
[6] If they still insist on making all the rules about visits, you may need to do something drastic like move farther away. No measure is too drastic if it means saving your marriage.

- ❏ We will chicken out and let them dictate when they will come to our house, how long they will stay, and where they will sleep.
- ❏ I will betray my wife by (a) letting my parents talk me out of the solution(s) we agreed upon and/or (b) blaming her for upsetting my parents.
- ❏ Other_____

Problem Issue #3: MOVING

My name is _____ and I am the husband. I would rather watch figure skating all day than fill out this worksheet, but I'm doing it anyway because I think it may lead to seeing my wife naked.

1. Whenever the topic of moving comes up, my wife does these things that make me want to force her to get a tattoo that reads, "I'm a jerk":
    - ❏ She says she doesn't want to live so close to my parents.
    - ❏ She says she hates it when my parents constantly drop by unexpectedly.
    - ❏ She complains that my parents intrude into our lives.
    - ❏ She says I spend too much time at my parents' house.
    - ❏ Other_____

2. If my parents were the bosses of the universe, these are the rules they would make about us moving away:
    - ❏ "Our son and his wife should live in the same town as us, even if they would prefer to move farther away."
    - ❏ "Our son and daughter-in-law should live close to us, even if it would be better for their marriage if there was some distance between us."
    - ❏ Other_____

3. If I were Boss of the Universe, these are the rules I would make about moving:
    - ❏ I would move to [a bigger town / the mountains].
    - ❏ My parents would support our decision to move farther away and assure us that they would get along fine without us.
    - ❏ My parents wouldn't accuse me of neglecting or abandoning them.
    - ❏ My wife and I would allow my parents to decide where we should live because our marriage isn't important.
    - ❏ Other_____

4. If I decided to be Mr. Loving Husband (instead of Boss of the Universe), I would consider some of the following compromises with my wife:
   ❑ "I want to live within 30 minutes of my parents, and you want to live in another state. How about if we move about four hours away from them?"
   ❑ "I want to live close to my parents and you want to live close to yours. How about if we move somewhere in between them?"
   ❑ "How about if for the next six months, (a) I/we will visit with my parents less often and (b) I'll start making your needs a priority over my parents' needs. After that trial run, we can evaluate whether or not it would be better for our marriage if we moved away."
   ❑ "I'm willing to _____
      if you're willing to _____."
      (For example: I'm willing to <u>quit working for my parents</u> if you're willing to <u>live here for at least another two years</u>.)
   ❑ Other_____

Stop now and read your compromises aloud to each other. Negotiate until you agree on a fair solution. Take breaks if you need to get your emotions under control or you need to get a fresh perspective. Write the agreed upon solution(s) here. _____
_____

Now discuss the next two questions until you can reach an agreement.

5. How will we communicate this decision to my parents[7]?
   ❑ I will call my parents and tell them that we have decided to move to a place where we have always wanted to live.
   ❑ We will tell my parents in person we have decided to move to [Montana].
   ❑ Other_____

Stop now and anticipate as a couple how your parents might react to your new behavior. (For instance, your dad might say, "Your mother will be devastated if you move away.")

---

[7] See the chapter entitled "Illegal Crack" (the section called 'Good Things To Say To Your Parents') for ideas on specific sentences to use with your parents.

6. Here's what we will do if my parents have a negative reaction[8]:

- ❏ I will be respectful and loving toward my parents, but I will stand firm and repeat our decision to them without backing down even if they are disappointed, hurt, or angry.
- ❏ I will hold strong to what my wife and I agreed upon even if my parents try to make me feel guilty, inconsiderate, selfish, or unloving for having needs that conflict with theirs.
- ❏ We will chicken out and let them dictate when they can visit us and where we should live.
- ❏ Other_____

---

[8] See the chapter entitled "Illegal Crack" (the section called 'Appropriate Things To Say If Your Parents Have A Bad Reaction') for specific sentences to use with your parents.

Problem Issue #4: <u>VISITS AT THEIR HOUSE</u>

My name is _____ and I am the husband. I would rather become a ballerina than fill out this worksheet, but I'm doing it anyway because I'm tired of my wife bugging me about it.

1. Whenever the topic of visiting my parents comes up, my wife does these things that make me wish I had married a goat:
   - ❑ She complains that we visit my parents too often.
   - ❑ She complains about having to stay at my parents' house for longer than a couple of days.
   - ❑ She is mean to my parents and me when we are at their house.
   - ❑ She says she wants to stay at a hotel instead of at my parents' house.
   - ❑ Other_____

2. If my parents were the bosses of the universe, these are the rules they would make about visits:
   - ❑ "Our son and his wife should come visit us even if it is expensive or inconvenient for them to do so."
   - ❑ "Our son and daughter-in-law should always stay at our house when they come to visit, even if they would prefer to stay at a hotel or with friends."
   - ❑ "Our son and his wife should always meet our expectations about how often they visit and how long they stay."
   - ❑ Other_____

3. If I were Boss of the Universe, these are the rules I would make about visits:
   - ❑ I would visit my parents when I *wanted* to instead of when I thought I *should.*
   - ❑ A typical visit with my parents would last [a couple of hours / a couple of days / a week].
   - ❑ My parents would take our needs into consideration instead of trying to make us feel guilty for not meeting their expectations.

❑ My wife and I would allow my parents to decide how often we should visit and how long we should stay, even though we are adults with needs of our own.

❑ Other_____

4. If I decided to be Mr. Loving Husband (instead of Boss of the Universe), I would consider some of the following compromises[9] with my wife:

❑ "I want to visit my parents for a week and you don't want to go at all. How about if we compromise and go for just the [day / weekend]?"

❑ "I want for us to go to my parents' house and you want them to come here instead. How about if we meet them halfway between our houses and stay at a hotel?"

❑ "I'm willing to _____
if you're willing to _____."
(For example: I'm willing to remodel your bedroom closet like you've been wanting if you're willing to spend a week at my parents' house next month.)

❑ Other_____

Stop now and read your compromises aloud to each other. Negotiate until you agree on a fair solution. Take breaks if you need to get your emotions under control or you need to get a fresh perspective. Write the agreed upon solution(s) here. _____

Now discuss the next two questions until you can reach an agreement.

5. How will we communicate this decision to my parents[10]?

❑ I will call my parents and respectfully tell them that we won't be able to visit them this [weekend / month / year] but that maybe we can get together with them next [weekend / month / year].

❑ I will e-mail my parents and let them know we plan to stay at a hotel (or with friends) when we come to visit.

❑ Other_____

---

[9] These compromises will vary depending on several factors such as how far away your parents live, whether or not you have kids, your work schedule, etc.

[10] See the chapter entitled "Illegal Crack" (specifically the section called 'Good Things To Say To Your Parents') for ideas on specific sentences to use with your parents.

Stop now and anticipate as a couple how your parents might react to your new behavior. (For instance, your mom might say, "Linda's son visits her every week. Why can't you be more like him?")

6. Here's what we will do if my parents have a negative reaction[11]:
   - ❑ We will tell them we won't come to visit at all if they continue to insist on being in charge of deciding how often we come or how long we stay.
   - ❑ We will chicken out and let them dictate how often we should visit them and how long we should stay.
   - ❑ Other_____

---

[11] See the chapter entitled "Illegal Crack" (specifically the section called 'Appropriate Things To Say If Your Parents Have A Bad Reaction') for specific sentences to use with your parents.

Problem Issue #5: <u>HOLIDAYS</u>

My name is _____ and I am the husband. I would rather run through a barbed wire fence than fill out this worksheet, but I'm doing it anyway because I'm a great husband.

1. Whenever the topic of holidays comes up, my wife does these things that make me want to fill her stocking with maggots:
   - ❏ She says she wants to spend Christmas at home with just the kids.
   - ❏ She says she doesn't want my parents to come to our house for Easter.
   - ❏ She says she doesn't want to go visit my parents for Thanksgiving.
   - ❏ Other_____

2. If my parents were the bosses of the universe, these are the rules they would make about holidays:
   - ❏ "Our son and his wife should spend Easter weekend with us even if they would prefer to do something else."
   - ❏ "Our son and his wife should come to our house for Thanksgiving even if they would rather have us over to their house instead."
   - ❏ "Our son and his wife should come see us for Christmas even if it is a big inconvenience and/or expense for them."
   - ❏ Other_____

3. If I were Boss of the Universe, these are the rules I would make about holidays:
   - ❏ My wife would ignore her needs in order to please my parents and/or me.
   - ❏ My parents wouldn't expect us to get together for every holiday.
   - ❏ My parents would come visit us sometimes instead of expecting us to go to the trouble and expense of visiting them.
   - ❏ My wife and I would decide as a couple where to spend each holiday without worrying about whether or not my parents approved.

❑ My wife and I would allow my parents to dictate where and when we should spend every holiday regardless of our feelings and needs.

❑ Other_____

4. If I decided to be Mr. Loving Husband (instead of Boss of the Universe), I would consider some of the following compromises[12] with my wife:

❑ "I'm willing to spend Christmas with your parents if you're willing to invite my parents here for Easter."

❑ "I'm willing to spend this Christmas at our house if you're willing to spend next Christmas at my parents' house."

❑ "Let's make a list of all of the holidays during the year and then barter and negotiate with each other until we decide where and with whom we are going to spend them."

❑ "I'm willing to _____ if you're willing to_____." (For example: I'm willing to <u>take you to that play you've been wanting to see</u> if you're willing to <u>go to my parents' house for Thanksgiving</u>.)

❑ Other_____

Stop now and read your compromises aloud to each other. Negotiate until you agree on a fair solution. Take breaks if you need to get your emotions under control or you need to get a fresh perspective. Write the agreed upon solution(s) here. _____

_____

Now discuss the next two questions until you can reach an agreement.

5. How will we communicate this decision to my parents[13]?

❑ I will call my parents and respectfully say what we've decided to do for the holidays.

❑ We will tell my parents in person what we've decided to do for the holidays.

_____

[12] These compromises will vary depending on several factors such as how far away your parents live, whether or not you have kids, your work schedule, etc.

[13] See the chapter entitled "Illegal Crack" (the section called 'Good Things To Say To Your Parents') for ideas on specific sentences to use with your parents.

❑   Other_____

Stop now and anticipate as a couple how your parents might react to your new behavior. (For instance, they might say, "But we always spend [Easter] together and it won't be the same without you.")

6. Here's what we will do if my parents have a negative reaction[14]:
    ❑   I will hold strong to what my wife and I agreed upon even if my parents try to make me feel guilty, inconsiderate, selfish, or unloving for having needs that conflict with theirs.
    ❑   We will chicken out and let them dictate where and with whom we should spend every holiday.
    ❑   I will betray my wife by (a) letting my parents talk me out of the solution(s) we agreed upon and/or (b) blaming her for upsetting my parents.

---

[14] See the chapter entitled "Illegal Crack" (the section called 'Appropriate Things To Say If Your Parents Have A Bad Reaction') for specific sentences to use with your parents.

Problem Issue #6: <u>VACATIONS</u>

My name is _____ and I am the husband. I would rather drill a hole in my head than fill out this worksheet, but I'm doing it anyway because I'm tired of fighting with my wife.

1. Whenever the topic of vacations comes up, my wife does these things that make me want to put piranhas in her bath water:
   - ❑ She says she doesn't want to spend our vacation with my parents.
   - ❑ She insists on spending our vacation with friends.
   - ❑ Other_____

2. If my parents were the bosses of the universe, these are the rules they would make about vacations:
   - ❑ "Our son and his wife should spend every vacation with us even if they would prefer to do something else."
   - ❑ "Our son and his wife should visit us once a year even though they have to use up all of their vacation time to do that."
   - ❑ Other_____

3. If I were Boss of the Universe, these are the rules I would make about vacations:
   - ❑ My wife and I would spend our vacation where and with whom we pleased, without worrying whether or not my parents approve.
   - ❑ Sometimes I would spend my vacation [camping with my wife and kids] or [going hunting with the guys from work] or [visiting the world's largest ball of twine].
   - ❑ My wife and I would let my parents dictate how we should use our vacation time even though we are adults.
   - ❑ Other_____

4. If I decided to be Mr. Loving Husband (instead of Boss of the Universe), I would consider some of the following compromises with my wife:
   - ❑ "How about if we spend half of our vacation with my parents and half with friends?"

- ❏ "I want to spend our vacation with my parents and you want to spend it with friends. How about if we compromise and spend this year's vacation with my parents and next year's vacation with friends?"
- ❏ "I'm willing to_____
  if you're willing to _____."
  (For example: I'm willing to <u>buy that dining set you've been wanting</u> if you're willing to <u>spend our vacation at my parents' house</u>.)
- ❏ Other_____

Stop now and read your compromises aloud to each other. Negotiate until you agree on a fair solution. Take breaks if you need to get your emotions under control or you need to get a fresh perspective. Write the agreed upon solution(s) here. _____
_____

Now discuss the next two questions until you can reach an agreement.

5. How will we communicate this decision to my parents[15]?
   - ❏ I will call my parents and respectfully tell them we've decided not to spend our vacation with them this year.
   - ❏ My wife will e-mail my parents and tell them we've decided to spend our vacation with her parents this year.
   - ❏ My wife and I will tell my parents in person we have decided to spend our vacation [in Colorado with friends].
   - ❏ Other_____

Stop now and anticipate as a couple how your parents might react to your new behavior. (For instance, they might say, "But we won't get to see you at all this year if you don't spend your vacation with us.")

---

[15] See the chapter entitled "Illegal Crack" (the section called 'Good Things To Say To Your Parents') for ideas on specific sentences to use with your parents.

6. Here's what we will do if my parents have a negative reaction[16]:
- ❑ I will be respectful and loving toward my parents, but I will stand firm and repeat our decision to them without backing down even if they are disappointed, hurt, and/or angry.
- ❑ We will chicken out and let them dictate where and with whom we should spend all our vacations.
- ❑ I will betray my wife by (a) letting my parents talk me out of the solution(s) we agreed upon and/or (b) blaming her for upsetting my parents.
- ❑ Other_____

---

[16] See the chapter entitled "Illegal Crack" (the section called 'Appropriate Things To Say If Your Parents Have A Bad Reaction') for specific sentences to use with your parents.

Problem Issue #7: TRADITIONS

My name is _____ and I am the husband. I would rather eat a box of thumbtacks than fill out this worksheet, but I'm doing it anyway because I love my wife (even though she belongs in an asylum).

1. Whenever the topic of traditions comes up, my wife does these things that make me want to shave her head while she's asleep:
    - ❏ She says she doesn't want to keep going to my parents' house every [Sunday] to [eat lunch with them].
    - ❏ She wants to start our own traditions instead of feeling obligated to follow my parents' traditions until we're old and gray.
    - ❏ Other_____

2. If my parents were the bosses of the universe, these are the rules they would make about traditions:
    - ❏ "Our son and his wife should meet with us every [Friday night] to [play cards] even if they would prefer to do something else with someone else."
    - ❏ "Our son and his wife should come to our house every [Sunday] for [lunch] even if they would prefer to meet somewhere else."
    - ❏ "Our son and his wife should always follow our traditions and never create their own."
    - ❏ Other_____

3. If I were Boss of the Universe, these are the rules I would make about traditions:
    - ❏ My wife and I would get together with my parents when we wanted to, instead of feeling obligated to stick to a rigid routine.
    - ❏ My wife and I would allow my parents to dictate our schedule, instead of being honest with them about our needs.
    - ❏ Other_____

253

4. If I decided to be Mr. Loving Husband (instead of Boss of the Universe), I would consider some of the following compromises[17] with my wife:
   - ❏ "It's fine with me if we stop meeting my parents every [Friday], but I don't have the courage to tell them. Would you?"
   - ❏ "I want to [watch football] with my parents on [Monday nights] and you don't. How about if I go to my folks' house on [Monday nights] while you go [hang out with your girlfriends]?"
   - ❏ "I'm willing to start a new tradition of taking you on a date once a month if you're willing to get together with my parents every other month."
   - ❏ Other_____

Stop now and read your compromises aloud to each other. Negotiate until you agree on a fair solution. Take breaks if you need to get your emotions under control or you need to get a fresh perspective. Write the agreed upon solution(s) here. _____

_____

Now discuss the next two questions until you can reach an agreement.

5. How will we communicate this decision to my parents[18]?
   - ❏ My wife will call my parents and tell them we can't get together this [Friday] to [play cards] and then ask if they would like to get together one day next month to see a movie.
   - ❏ When my parents invite us to come over to their house for [dinner] on [Saturday], I'll suggest meeting at a restaurant instead.
   - ❏ Other_____

Stop now and anticipate as a couple how your parents might react to your new behavior. (For instance, your mom might say, "I guess you just don't have time for us anymore.")

---

[17] These compromises will vary depending on several factors such as how far away your parents live, whether or not you have kids, your work schedule, etc.

[18] See the chapter entitled "Illegal Crack" (the section called 'Good Things To Say To Your Parents') for ideas on specific sentences to use with your parents.

6. Here's what we will do if my parents have a negative reaction[19]:

- ❏ I will be respectful and loving toward my parents, but I will stand firm and repeat our needs to them without backing down even if they are disappointed, hurt, or angry.
- ❏ We will chicken out and let them dictate when and where we should get together and what activity we should do at that time.
- ❏ I will betray my wife by (a) letting my parents talk me out of the solution(s) we agreed upon and/or (b) blaming her for upsetting my parents.
- ❏ Other_____

---

[19] See the chapter entitled "Illegal Crack" (the section called 'Appropriate Things To Say If Your Parents Have A Bad Reaction') for specific sentences to use with your parents.

Problem Issue #8: <u>ADVICE</u>

My name is _____ and I am the husband. I would rather eat a bowl of dirt than fill out this worksheet, but I'm doing it anyway because otherwise my wife won't leave me alone.

1. Whenever the topic of advice comes up, my wife does these things that make me want to tie her to a tree covered with army ants:
   - ❏ She hates it when my parents advise us on how we should spend our time and money.
   - ❏ She gets furious when my parents interfere with our decisions.
   - ❏ She asks me to stop giving my parents details about our [finances] and [sex life].
   - ❏ Other_____

2. If my parents were the bosses of the universe, these are the rules they would make about advice:
   - ❏ "Our son and his wife should never make a decision without first asking us what they should do."
   - ❏ "Our son and his wife should always take our advice about everything (even though they are adults who are capable of making their own decisions)."
   - ❏ "Our son and his wife should share details of their [finances] and [sex life] with us."
   - ❏ Other_____

3. If I were Boss of the Universe, these are the rules I would make about advice:
   - ❏ My parents wouldn't give advice about how I should spend my time and money.
   - ❏ My wife and I would make decisions about how to spend our time and money without worrying whether or not my parents approve.
   - ❏ My parents would only offer advice when we ask for it.
   - ❏ My wife and I would let my parents make all of our decisions even though we have the right to make our own choices and the responsibility to accept the consequences.
   - ❏ Other_____

4. If I decided to be Mr. Loving Husband (instead of Boss of the Universe), I would consider some of the following compromises with my wife:
   - ❑ "How about if I stop asking for my parents' advice about everything and you stop complaining that they give too much advice?"
   - ❑ "I'll try to start seeking the advice of other people instead of always relying on my parents to help me make decisions. In exchange, I'd like for you to be open to hearing their advice when it comes to subjects that they are knowledgeable about."
   - ❑ Other_____

Stop now and read your compromises aloud to each other. Negotiate until you agree on a fair solution. Take breaks if you need to get your emotions under control or you need to get a fresh perspective. Write the agreed upon solution(s) here. _____

_____

Now discuss the next two questions until you can reach an agreement.

5. How will we communicate this decision to my parents[20]?
   - ❑ I'll stop asking for my parents' advice about everything and instead I'll only ask for their advice occasionally.
   - ❑ We'll start making decisions as a couple even if my parents don't approve.
   - ❑ We'll avoid bringing up topics that tend to make my parents offer advice.
   - ❑ The next time my parents pressure us to take their advice, I'll say "Thanks for your input but we've decided to do something else."
   - ❑ The next time my parents ask me about [our finances] or [sex life], I'll say, "That's something we'd like to keep private."
   - ❑ Other_____

Stop now and anticipate as a couple how your parents might react to your new behavior. (For instance, they might say, "We are just trying to help you.")

_____

[20] See the chapter entitled "Illegal Crack" (the section called 'Good Things To Say To Your Parents') for ideas on specific sentences to use with your parents.

6. Here's what we will do if my parents have a negative reaction[21]:

- ❑ We will be respectful and loving toward my parents, but we will make our own decisions even if they are disappointed, hurt, or angry with us for doing so.
- ❑ I will hold strong to what my wife and I agreed upon even if my parents try to make us feel guilty, inconsiderate, selfish or unloving for not accepting their advice.
- ❑ We will apologize profusely even though we have done nothing wrong.
- ❑ We will chicken out and let them make all of our decisions for us.
- ❑ Other_____

---

[21] See the chapter entitled "Illegal Crack" (the section called 'Appropriate Things To Say If Your Parents Have A Bad Reaction') for specific sentences to use with your parents.

Problem Issue #9: <u>FINANCIAL INDEPENDENCE</u>

My name is _____ and I am the husband. I would rather eat a spider than fill out this worksheet, but I'm doing it anyway because I'm tired of hearing my wife nag me about being financially dependent on my parents.

1. Whenever the topic of financial independence comes up, my wife does these things that make me want to burn all of her shoes:
   ❑ She complains about having to live in my parents' house.
   ❑ She says she doesn't want my parents to watch our kids every day.
   ❑ She pressures me to stop working for my parents.
   ❑ Other_____

2. If my parents were the bosses of the universe, these are the rules they would make about our finances:
   ❑ "Our son and his wife should remain financially dependent on us even though they are capable of providing for themselves."
   ❑ "Our son should continue to work for us even if he would rather work elsewhere."
   ❑ "Our son and daughter-in-law should let us make the decisions about who should provide their childcare even though they are the parents."
   ❑ Other_____

3. If I were Boss of the Universe, these are the rules I would make about our finances:
   ❑ My wife and I would become financially independent from my parents.
   ❑ My wife and I would remain financially dependent on my parents for the rest of our lives.
   ❑ I would stop working for my parents and look for a job I loved.
   ❑ I would work for my parents for the rest of my life even though (a) it causes tension in my marriage and (b) I'd rather work elsewhere.

- ❑ We would not accept money or a gift from my parents if it were given with the intent to control us.
- ❑ My wife and I would allow ourselves to be controlled by my parents' money and/or gifts.
- ❑ My wife and I would decide who would provide childcare, and my parents would respect our decision.
- ❑ My wife and I would allow my parents to decide who should provide childcare, even though it's our decision and our children.
- ❑ Other_____

4. If I decided to be Mr. Loving Husband (instead of Boss of the Universe), I would consider some of the following compromises with my wife:
   - ❑ "I'm willing to pay my parents what we owe them if you're willing to pick up some overtime shifts at work for the next couple of months."
   - ❑ "If you're willing to live with my parents for one more month, I'm willing to go with you to look for a place of our own."
   - ❑ "I'll start looking for another job if you stop saying my parents are controlling."
   - ❑ Other_____

Stop now and read your compromises aloud to each other. Negotiate until you agree on a fair solution. Take breaks if you need to get your emotions under control or you need to get a fresh perspective. Write the agreed upon solution(s) here. _____
_____

Now discuss the next two questions until you can reach an agreement.

5. How will we communicate this decision to my parents[22]?
   - ❑ We will pay my parents the money we owe them and then use banks for future loans.
   - ❑ I will respectfully tell my parents we will be moving out of their house at the end of the month.

---

[22] See the chapter entitled "Illegal Crack" (specifically the section called 'Good Things To Say To Your Parents') for ideas on specific sentences to use with your parents.

- ❑ When my parents give us money or a gift with strings attached, we will clarify their motives and then decide whether or not to accept it.
- ❑ My wife will call my parents and tell them we have decided to change our daycare arrangements.
- ❑ Other_____

Stop now and anticipate as a couple how your parents might react to your new behavior. (For instance, they might say, "You should just be grateful for our money and gifts instead of refusing to accept our help.")

6. Here's what we will do if my parents have a negative reaction[23]:
- ❑ I will hold strong to what my wife and I agreed upon even if my parents try to make us feel guilty, ungrateful, or rude for wanting financial independence.
- ❑ Other_____

---

[23] See the chapter entitled "Illegal Crack" (specifically the section called 'Appropriate Things To Say If Your Parents Have A Bad Reaction') for specific sentences to use with your parents.

Problem Issue #10: <u>CHILDREN</u>

My name is _____ and I am the husband. I would rather take a knitting class than fill out this worksheet, but I'm doing it anyway because my wife is very persuasive.

1. Whenever the topic of children comes up, my wife does these things that make me want to throw a dirty diaper at her:
    - ❑ She gets really mad at my parents when they offer advice or criticize our parenting decisions.
    - ❑ She refuses to take their advice.
    - ❑ She gets mad at me when I let my parents decide how we should raise our kids (such as what religion they should be taught, how they should dress, and how they should be disciplined).
    - ❑ She hates it when my folks compete with her parents for their grandchild's love and attention (by buying expensive gifts and/or complaining that the other grandparents get to see the kids more often than they do).
    - ❑ She complains every time my parents drop by to see the kids.
    - ❑ She gets furious when my parents refuse to observe the rules we have for our kids (such as what they can eat, how much TV they can watch, and bedtime).
    - ❑ She hates it when my parents tell me things that imply she's not a very good mother (such as "I don't think she dressed the baby warm enough" or "breast feeding is much healthier than bottle feeding").
    - ❑ Other_____

2. If my parents were the bosses of the universe, these are the rules they would make about their grandkids:
    - ❑ "We are entitled to visit our grandkids whenever we want to, even if it interferes with the needs of our son and his wife."
    - ❑ "We have the right to make all of the parenting decisions (discipline methods, religious upbringing, etc.) about our grandkids even though we are not the parents."
    - ❑ "We can ignore the rules our son and his wife have set for their kids."

❏   "We should get to see our grandkids just as much or more than the other set of grandparents get to see them."

❏   Other_____

3. If I were Boss of the Universe, these are the rules I would make about our kids:

❏   My wife and I would make parenting decisions as a couple without worrying whether or not my parents approved.

❏   My parents would support our parenting methods instead of offering constant advice.

❏   My parents wouldn't criticize the way we raise our kids.

❏   My parents would encourage our kids to respect our authority by observing the rules we have for them.

❏   My parents would wait for an invitation or at least call before dropping by to see their grandkids.

❏   My parents would behave maturely instead of engaging in childish competition with the other set of grandparents.

❏   Other_____

4. If I decided to be Mr. Loving Husband (instead of Boss of the Universe), I would consider some of the following compromises with my wife:

❏   "I'll stop insisting that we follow my parents' advice if you stop complaining that they give too much advice."

❏   "I'm willing to tell my parents to stop criticizing our parenting methods if you're willing to stop criticizing my parents in front of the kids."

❏   "I'm willing to talk to my folks about observing our rules if you're willing to let them spend time with the kids next weekend."

❏   "If you're willing to speak to my parents in a respectful tone, I'll back you up when you tell them that they need to wait for an invitation before they show up."

❏   "I'm willing to talk to my folks about competing over the kids if you're willing to talk to your folks about it too."

❏   Other_____

Stop now and read your compromises aloud to each other. Negotiate until you agree on a fair solution. Take breaks if you need to get your emotions under control or you need to get a fresh perspective. Write the agreed upon solution(s) here. _____

_____

Now discuss the next two questions until you can reach an agreement, write down the solutions you've agreed on, and read the solutions aloud to each other.

5. How will we communicate this decision to my parents[24]?
    - ❑ I will stop discussing parenting issues with my folks.
    - ❑ We'll tell my folks that we expect them to respect the rules we have for our kids and that there will be consequences if they don't.
    - ❑ If my parents criticize our parenting methods in front of our kids, then I will give them a warning. If they do it again, I will either leave (with the kids) or ask them to leave.
    - ❑ I will ask my parents to stop [giving our kids expensive gifts] or [keeping track of which grandparents get to see our kids more].
    - ❑ I will tell my folks that I'm not willing to listen to them criticize my wife behind her back and that in the future I expect them to confront her directly.
    - ❑ Other_____

Stop now and anticipate as a couple how your parents might react to your new behavior. (For instance, they might say, "You would be wise to listen to our advice because we have more experience raising kids than you do.")

6. Here's what we will do if my parents have a negative reaction[25]:
    - ❑ We will stand firm and follow through on our parenting decisions even if they don't approve or they try to make us feel guilty, disrespectful, or foolish for not taking their advice.

---

[24] See the chapter entitled "Illegal Crack" (the section called 'Good Things To Say To Your Parents') for ideas on specific sentences to use with your parents.

[25] See the chapter entitled "Illegal Crack" (specifically the section called 'Appropriate Things To Say If Your Parents Have A Bad Reaction') for specific sentences to use with your parents.

❑   We will restate our needs (about visits, rules, gossip, competitiveness, etc.) again without backing down even if they get upset.
❑   We will let them decide how to raise our kids even though we are the parents.
❑   Other_____

Problem Issue #11: <u>ELDER CARE</u>

My name is _____ and I am the husband. I would rather have my limbs removed than fill out this worksheet, but I'm doing it anyway so my wife won't bug me until the day I die.

1. Whenever the topic of taking care of my elderly parents comes up, my wife does these things that make me want to put *her* into a nursing home:
   - ❑ She refuses to let my parents come live with us.
   - ❑ She complains that I spend too much time taking care of my parents.
   - ❑ She says she doesn't have time or energy to take care of my parents by herself.
   - ❑ She accuses my parents of exaggerating their illnesses to manipulate us.
   - ❑ She wants to move my parents to a place where they can get the professional care they need.
   - ❑ Other_____

2. If my parents were the bosses of the universe, these are the rules they would make about their elder care:
   - ❑ "Our son and his wife should be our primary caregivers even if they don't have the time, energy, or knowledge required to do so."
   - ❑ "Our son and daughter-in-law should let us move in with them even if they don't have room."
   - ❑ "Our son and his wife should neglect their marriage, kids, careers, social lives, health, housework, and yard work in order to take care of us."
   - ❑ Other_____

3. If I were Boss of the Universe, these are the rules I would make about taking care of my elderly parents:
   - ❑ My parents wouldn't insist we do things for them that they are perfectly capable of doing for themselves.

- ❑ I would help my parents with the things I wanted to help with, and then hire professionals to help them with the things I don't want to help with.
- ❑ My parents would be willing to consider all of the elder care options available and realize our needs are just as important as theirs.
- ❑ My wife and I would allow my parents to guilt us into neglecting our own needs in order to tend to all of theirs.
- ❑ Other_____

4. If I decided to be Mr. Loving Husband (instead of Boss of the Universe), I would consider some of the following compromises[26] with my wife:
   - ❑ "I'm willing to drive my mom to the doctor this week if you're willing to take her next week."
   - ❑ "If you're willing to call my parents every afternoon to see if they are okay, then I'm willing to check on them every morning and ask the kids to check on them every evening."
   - ❑ "If you're willing to take my dad grocery shopping on Fridays then I'm willing to pick up the kids from school."
   - ❑ "I'm willing to take you on a vacation if you're willing to find a reputable elder care facility where we can leave my parents for a week."
   - ❑ "I'm willing to take my folks to an adult daycare center on Tuesdays and Thursdays if you're willing to take care of them on Mondays, Wednesdays, and Fridays."
   - ❑ "I'm willing to go with you to talk to a geriatric care manager and/or physician about where my parents should live, if you are willing to schedule an appointment with someone reputable."
   - ❑ "I'm willing to read a book about elder care if you're willing to find a good one for me."
   - ❑ Other_____

---

[26] These compromises will vary depending on several factors such as how far away your parents live, whether or not you have kids, your work schedule, etc.

Stop now and read your compromises aloud to each other. Negotiate until you agree on a fair solution. Take breaks if you need to get your emotions under control or you need to get a fresh perspective. Write the agreed upon solution(s) here. _____

_____

Now discuss the next two questions until you can reach an agreement.

5. How will we communicate this decision to my parents[27]?
   - ❏ I will call my dad and tell him that I will take him to the grocery store this week and that I have asked his neighbor Eileen to take him next week.
   - ❏ I will call my mom and let her know that I won't be coming over this weekend to do her yard work, but that I hired a boy in her neighborhood to start mowing her lawn (or shoveling snow from her driveway).
   - ❏ I will visit my parents and make their house safe for them so they can enjoy their independence for as long as possible (instead of moving them into our house or a nursing home).
   - ❏ My wife and I will visit my folks and ask them whether they would prefer to move to an assisted living facility or have us hire a homecare worker to come live with them.
   - ❏ My wife and I will tell them we'd like to take them to visit a nice place (an adult home) where they could meet new friends, get to do fun activities, *and* have someone else do the cooking for them.
   - ❏ Other_____

Stop now and anticipate as a couple how your parents might react to your new behavior. (For instance your mom might say, "Be a good son and let me move in with you so that I won't be so lonely.")

6. Here's what we will do if my parents have a negative reaction[28]:
   - ❏ I will be respectful and loving toward my parents, but I will stand my ground even if they are disappointed, hurt, or angry.

---

[27] See the chapter entitled "Illegal Crack" (the section called 'Good Things To Say To Your Parents') for ideas on specific sentences to use with your parents.
[28] See the chapter entitled "Illegal Crack" (the section called 'Appropriate Things To Say If Your Parents Have A Bad Reaction') for specific sentences to use with your parents.

- ❏ I will hold strong to what my wife and I agreed upon even if my parents try to make me feel guilty, inconsiderate, selfish, or unloving for having needs that conflict with theirs.
- ❏ We will cave under pressure and agree to all of their demands even if it destroys our marriage, health, and social life.
- ❏ Other_____

Conclusion

The best way to predict the future is to invent it.
                                        --Unknown

Wives, I won't lie to you…gaining your husband's loyalty won't be easy. Take a minute to think of the most difficult thing you have ever done in your entire life. Now multiply that by 32 and you'll have an idea of how hard it can be to gain your husband's loyalty. For instance, if your most challenging accomplishment was the time you gave birth to triplets while getting a root canal, then multiply that times 32. In order for you to accomplish such a huge goal, you need to learn how to love your husband more than you dislike his parents. You're a smart person, so I'm sure you realize that, when I say you're going to need love for your husband in order to get through this, I'm not talking about just a small piece of love. I am talking about a humongous chunk of love that won't even fit through the front door of most residential homes.

Only you can change your life. Visualize a future you want and hold tight to that dream until it comes true. My marriage survived difficult in-laws and yours can too!

If this book was helpful to you, please recommend it to a friend so her marriage can grow stronger too. (Refer her to my website at www.WifeGuide.org.)

If this book made your marriage stronger, please e-mail me your success story at wifeguide@yahoo.com. Let me know if I can post it on my website to inspire other wives. I promise to change the names in order to protect the identities of everyone involved.

If you are a marriage therapist or premarital counselor who agrees with the ideas in this book, please recommend it to your clients and colleagues. As a thank you, I would love to recommend your name on my website. Please contact me at wifeguide@yahoo.com with your contact information and a note saying "Please add me to your referral list."

ABOUT THE AUTHOR

Married 14 years, Jenna D. Barry (a pen name) learned how to gain her husband's loyalty through communication, persistence, and a whole lot of love. She familiarized herself with the needs and frustrations of other wives by participating in on-line in-law support groups and by talking to marriage therapists, friends, family, and co-workers. She then started her own positive, encouraging support group for wives and created a website about in-laws at www.WifeGuide.org.

Jenna's book has been endorsed by many marriage professionals. She has done radio interviews, and her articles have been published in various websites and magazines, including Hitched Magazine, Mom Magazine, Families On-line Magazine, TheNest.com, Pregnancy.org, ForeverBrides.com, CanadianParents.com, About.com, and MarriedRomance.com.

RECOMMENDED BOOKS

- <u>Toxic In-laws: Loving Strategies for Protecting your Marriage</u> by Susan Forward
- <u>Do Your Parents Drive You Crazy? : A Survival Guide for Adult Children</u> by Janet Dight
- <u>Six in the Bed: Dealing with Parents, In-laws, and Their Impact on Your Marriage</u> by Nancy Wasserman Cocola
- <u>The Mom Factor : Dealing With the Mother You Had, Didn't Have, or Still Contend With</u> by Henry Cloud and John Townsend
- <u>Boundaries: When to Say Yes, When to Say No, To Take Control of Your Life</u> by Henry Cloud and John Townsend
- <u>Boundaries Face to Face: How to Have That Difficult Conversation You've Been Avoiding</u> by Henry Cloud and John Townsend
- <u>If You Had Controlling Parents: How to Make Peace with your Past and Take your Place in the World</u> by Dan Neuharth
- <u>The Emotionally Abusive Relationship: How to Stop Being Abused and How to Stop Abusing</u> by Beverly Engel
- <u>When Anger Hurts Your Relationship</u> by Kim Paleg, Ph.D. and Matthew McKay, Phd.
- <u>Babyproofing Your Marriage: How to Laugh More, Argue Less, and Communicate Better As Your Family Grows</u> by Stacy Cockrell, Cathy O'Neill, and Julia Stone
- <u>Eldercare 911: The Caregiver's Complete Handbook for Making Decisions</u> by Susan Beerman, M.S., MS.W. and Judith Rappaport-Musson
- <u>Helping Your Aging Parent: A Step-By-Step Guide</u> by William J. Grote

Made in the USA
Lexington, KY
03 October 2011